H

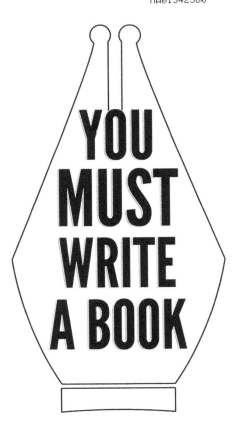

BOOST YOUR BRAND, GET MORE BUSINESS, AND BECOME THE GO-TO EXPERT

FOREWORD BY HAL ELROD,
BESTSELLING AUTHOR OF *THE MIRACLE MORNING*

ALSO BY HONORÉE CORDER

Like a Boss book series

Write Like a Boss: From a Whisper to a Roar

Publish Like a Boss: From Mind to Market

Market Like a Boss: From Book to Blockbuster

I Must Write My Book: The Companion Workbook to You Must Write a Book

The Prosperous Writer book series

Prosperity for Writers: A Writer's Guide to Creating Abundance

Prosperity for Writer's Productivity Journal

The Nifty 15: Write Your Book in Just 15 Minutes a Day!

The Prosperous Writer's Guide to Making More Money: Habits, Tactics, and Strategies for Making a Living as a Writer

The Prosperous Writer's Guide to Finding Readers: Build Your Author Brand, Raise Your Profile and Find Readers to Delight

Business Dating: Applying Relationship Rules in Business for Ultimate Success

Tall Order: Organize Your Life and Double Your Success in Half the Time

Vision to Reality: How Short Term Massive Action Equals Long Term Maximum Results

The Divorced Phoenix: Rising from the Ashes of a Broken Marriage

If Divorce is a Game, These are the Rules: 8 Rules for Thriving Before, During and After Divorce

The Successful Single Mom book series

The Miracle Morning book series

Published by Honorée Enterprises Publishing

Copyright 2019 © Honorée Enterprises Publishing

All rights reserved. No part of this book may be reproduced or transmitted in any form or by any means, electronic or mechanical, including photocopying, recording or by any information storage and retrieval system without written permission of the publisher, except for the inclusion of brief quotations in a review.

Cover design: Dino Marino & Interior design: Dino Marino

Tradepaper ISBN: 978-1-947665-09-5
Digital ISBN: 978-1-947665-10-1

March 2019

SPECIAL INVITATION

I'd like to personally invite you to join the Prosperity for Writers Mastermind at HonoreeCorder.com/Writers and Facebook.com/groups/ProsperityforWriters where you will find motivation, daily support, and help with any writing or self-publishing questions.

You can connect with me personally on Twitter @Honoree, or on Facebook.com/Honoree. Thank you so much for your most precious resource, your time. I look forward to connecting and hearing about your book soon!

> **BE SURE TO SIGN UP FOR INSTANT ACCESS FOR ALL THE PUBLISHING RESOURCES I INCLUDE IN THIS BOOK!**
> Just visit: www.HonoreeCorder.com/youmustbonuses

TABLE OF CONTENTS

FOREWORD
    by Hal Elrod.. ix

CHAPTER ONE
    Writing a Book Is the Best Thing
    You Can Do for Your Business... 1

CHAPTER TWO
    Who Must Write a Book? 11

CHAPTER THREE
    Why Write a Book? 20

CHAPTER FOUR
    Pre-Book Strategic Thinking:
    Before You Write Your Book 3 29

CHAPTER FIVE
    How to Write Your Book 40

CHAPTER SIX
    How You Can Self-Publish Your Book 58

CHAPTER SEVEN
    You Must Launch Your Book Like a Champ........................72

CHAPTER EIGHT
    You Must Plan to Market Your Book...................................93

CHAPTER NINE
    You Must Market Your Book..105

CHAPTER TEN
    You Must Market *with* Your Book.......................................117

CHAPTER ELEVEN
    You're in Great Company...138

CHAPTER TWELVE
    You Must Write a Book
    and You Must Get Started Now...146

END OF BOOK STUFF...155

QUICK FAVOR..158

GRATITUDE..159

WHO IS HONORÉE CORDER 161

Why You Must Write a Book

Foreword by Hal Elrod
Author of *The Miracle Morning*

"But I'm not a writer. Shoot, I could barely write an essay when I was in college, let alone a book" was my response.

"Did you graduate from high school? Do you know how to use a computer? Then you know how to write a book" was his. A bit snarky, but I got his point.

He followed it up with some compelling logic: "Look, the fact is that writing a book is now one of the best ways to become an authority in your field, attract new clients, and grow your business. Having a book will enable you to significantly increase your fees, create an additional ongoing passive income stream from book royalties, and cement the legacy you leave long after you're gone. And you don't have to be a good writer to do that; you just need to hire a good editor. Heck, you can even hire a ghostwriter."

It was hard to argue with that logic, so I didn't. Instead, I decided I would figure out how to write a book—even though I wasn't a writer.

FOREWORD BY HAL ELROD

Fifteen years and seven books later, I can tell you that, without question, writing and self-publishing a book was the best decision I've ever made—for me, my family, and my business—adding over $500,000 in annual revenue from book royalties, which is almost pure profit, each year.

However, making the decision to write a book is one that involved overcoming the following insecurities, limiting beliefs, and hurdles—some of which you may be facing:

- I am not a (good) writer.
- I don't have time to write a book.
- I don't know how to write a book.
- I don't know what to write about.
- What if no one buys my book? Or worse ...
- What if no one likes my book?

In the words of George McFly, "I don't think I can take that kind of rejection."

Luckily, Honorée Corder has written *the* book that will ensure that you can easily overcome all the hurdles listed above, and anything else that might be holding you back.

I know, because Honorée has helped me to write, publish, and launch five of my seven books and to make every single one of them a #1 best seller. Actually, "helped" is a gross understatement. She has been largely responsible for nearly every aspect of those five books being written, published, and continuing to generate ongoing sales and royalties month after month for several years with no end in sight.

You could say that Honorée Corder is my *secret weapon for book writing, publishing, and sales success*. What's exciting is that now she's *your* secret weapon, too!

In fact, I don't think there is a person on earth more uniquely qualified to teach you how to use a self-published book to boost your brand, get more business, and become the go-to expert in your field than Honorée. Author of dozens of books (or so, I can't keep track anymore), co-creator of the best-selling Miracle Morning book series, and coach to other best-selling authors, Honorée has condensed her decades of experience and simplified everything you need into a book that you can easily follow to become a best-selling author in a way that grows your business.

What I've realized is that writing a book is like any other business undertaking that provides huge rewards but is out of our comfort zone: When we know someone who has successfully *been there and done that*, and who is offering to show us the way, we simply have to accept their assistance.

You don't have to be a good writer, know how to write a book, or even (at this point) know what you are going to write about. You only need an open mind and the willingness to implement the steps that Honorée is about to share with you … Because 95 percent of your competition probably never will!

—Hal Elrod, author of *The Miracle Morning*
www.MiracleMorning.com

Dear Professional,

I truly believe almost everyone in business should write a book. As you might already suspect, your business card just doesn't cut it anymore. Saying you're *the best* at what you do falls on deaf ears. A shiny website doesn't hold the same allure it once did. Even the luster once held by advanced degrees has dulled.

The one thing that holds more cachet than almost anything else is being an author.

I know this firsthand as I've written multiple books to share my knowledge while simultaneously expanding my reach, brand identity, and, of course, my income.

I say this with every ounce of my being: it is high time you wrote your business book. You know, the one you've contemplated writing, procrastinated starting, and realize you probably should write.

As an experienced businessperson, you can write a book to gain clients or customers, develop professional relationships, get hired for speaking gigs, and even build your legacy. Just getting started in the business world? Writing a book puts you head and shoulders above the other thousand candidates who are applying for the same jobs you are and at the same time establishes your credibility like nothing else can.

You might have it in your mind that writing and publishing a book can be difficult or next to impossible. You're not wrong, yet it's easier than you think to become an author.

Yes, you absolutely should write your book. In fact, I think *You Must Write a Book!*

And you know it, too, don't you? In a world where everyone who does what you do also says the same things you say, there is one differentiator left that leaves no doubt you are the hands-down choice.

Hint: you're holding one in your hands.

Yes, ladies and gentlemen, you, too, must write a book.

What's holding you back? I think I know … Writing a book is hard. You're not qualified, or you don't think your opinion differs from what else is available. There's not another minute you could squeeze out of your already overpacked days.

I've heard every reason for not writing a book, and yet I know writing a book will change your life. You'll make more money. You'll impact more lives. You'll leave a legacy.

How do you go from today (no book) to published (Here's my book!)? Keep reading, it's all in here.

I wrote *You Must Write a Book* to tell you many of the reasons *why* YOU must write a book, *when* and *how* to get it written, *why* you definitely should self-publish it, and *how* to make sure you do it in the most professional way possible.

With this book as your guide, writing a book is no longer a daunting or impossible task. You'll write and publish it in record time, and it will help you achieve the goals you haven't even thought big enough to set just yet.

I suggest that you read through the whole book, and then go through it and execute it step-by-step. I've even created a companion workbook for you, *I Must Write My Book*. What are we waiting for? I'm ready when you are. Let's do this!

Honorée Corder
Author, Coach, Speaker, Wife, Mom, Optimist

— 1 —
WRITING A BOOK IS THE BEST THING YOU CAN DO FOR YOUR BUSINESS

*Someone doesn't want your business card,
they want your book.*

—JEFFREY GITOME

I believe with my whole heart and soul that you must write a book. A successful professional you might just be (and probably are), but without a book, you are likely perceived as someone who does what many other people do.

How would a prospective client know the difference between you and the 37 other people they've met in the past week with the same elevator pitch? What is the one thing you do differently? How are you better than your closest competition or the person who says they are, in fact, a better choice than you?

Well, probably nothing.

Your testimonials say you're great. Your business card is wonderful, but with all due respect, it is a piece of trash waiting to happen. Your LinkedIn profile is terrific, except LinkedIn highlights the other people with your exact qualifications in the sidebar.

You must add a tool to your toolbox most others don't know to have or aren't willing to create. What is this one thing that can separate you from the crowd and convince a prospect to sign on the dotted line to engage you instead of someone else? Of course we both know: *a book*.

Not just any book, either. Your book. The book in which you pour your knowledge, education, and expertise combined with your unique perspective and engaging sense of humor.

How do I know all this is true, and why should you listen to me?

While this isn't about me, I won't be able to convince you that writing a book is one of the most important and life-changing business moves you can make without sharing some of my story.

I have been a business and executive coach for more than twenty years. My clients are celebrities, high-profile entrepreneurs, senior-level professionals and executives, attorneys, financial professionals, and CEOs of the Fortune 500. The highest of the highest paid. And yet, that wasn't always the case. I was a garden variety business coach, at least according to perception, charging a common business coach fee until I had been coaching for a half-dozen years.

Then I wrote a book.

It wasn't until I wrote *Tall Order! Organize Your Life and Double Your Success in Half the Time* and added author to my list of credentials that my coaching practice, and my fees, shifted into high gear.

Writing a book wasn't in my business plan. In fact, I had never taken a writing class, nor had I studied creative writing or even journalism in college (a practical impossibility, as I never attended college). I certainly didn't consider myself a writer! I met Mark Victor Hansen, coauthor of the best-selling *Chicken Soup for the Soul* book series, at a conference in 2004. When he asked me what I did, I proudly said, "I am a business coach and a speaker."

To which he responded, "That's nice, honey. Everyone is a coach and a speaker. You must write a book!"

I wryly thought, *Well, how hard could that be?*

I gave him the blank look I see when I suggest to someone that they, too, must write a book. I'm lucky he took my silence as a license to continue. He said, "Do you have a speech you've given that's popular?"

I answered, "Yes, I have a speech titled *Master Strategies for Explosive Business Growth*."

He said, "Take that speech and write it down, word for word. Let that be the basis of your book."

At the time my daughter was four years old. I was a single mom with a high school education and building my coaching and speaking business. I worked from 4:00–6:30 a.m. (before she woke up in the morning), from 8:30 a.m.–2:35 p.m. (while she was in preschool), and most nights from 7:30–11:00 p.m. (after she went to bed and until I couldn't keep my eyes open). Of course, in my mind, I had several viable reasons why I could not write a book.

I chose to focus on the gift that was Mark's advice: *you must write a book*.

As it turns out, writing a book wasn't actually *that* hard. Don't misunderstand me, I'm not saying it was, or is, easy ... but it is doable! Most importantly, *writing my first book is the single best thing I ever did for my career.* I think it probably will be the most important action you will ever take for your career, and that's why I wrote this book.

Let's get back to the story of my first book: I had a wonderful friend who volunteered to have my daughter stay at her house for the weekend so I could write. From Friday morning until Sunday afternoon, I turned my speech into words on paper. I got up from my chair only to make more green tea and eat. It was grueling. It was challenging. *It was worth it.*

By the end of the weekend, I had a rough draft. I also had a book project I never wanted to look at again. You know what they say, too much of something is just too much! I let the manuscript marinate for a few weeks, and then I hired a coach, Jeff Sloan, cofounder of StartupNation. He was someone I admired, and it was of particular interest to me that he had recently published his first book. The mission of our work together was simple: help me figure out if I had a "good book" on my hands, and, if so, get it published.

With no education or other interesting credentials, I never entertained trying to secure a book deal. As it turns out, this was a blessing in disguise! (More on that later.) Jeff read my manuscript in preparation for our session, and I'll never forget the surprise I heard in his voice when we spoke. "Your book is actually really good! Now let's get it published!"

That first book, *Tall Order!,* provided the credibility a business card, brochure, or website could not. Prospective clients and business connections could get a taste of my approach, humor, and style without having to invest more than the cost of a few cups of coffee. Those who liked what I had to say and how I said it, chose to hire me. And, I suppose, the opposite is also true.

Since I wrote *Tall Order!*, the 10th anniversary edition of which was released in 2015, my calendar has been filled with clients' appointments. Why? Because while other coaches, speakers, and trainers all said pretty much the same thing, I had a book. And I was the one who was hired. Even though I doubled my fee shortly after the book was published, pricing me far above what other coaches were charging, I had a waiting list of clients. Bonus: I attracted higher quality clients, who were willing and able to pay more.

So yes, having a book is going to increase the likelihood you'll engage more business with higher quality clients at a higher fee. But wait, there's more …

I presold 11,000 copies of the book before I ever had the first copy in my hot little hands (you can read more about this at HonoreeCorder.com/11000) and have since sold tens of thousands of copies of *Tall Order!* alone, adding an additional income stream to my bottom line.

Speaking of additional streams of income, having a book led to paid keynote presentations and corporate training within the first year after the book was released. In the last decade, I have expanded my offerings to include online courses, consulting, coach certification, and so much more.

Eventually, I was inspired to write more books. When I expanded my catalog to include what is now the Successful Single Mom book series, I was led to and made even more incredible connections and opportunities.

But making more money isn't the best aspect of having a book. I've saved the best for last: having books has allowed me to positively impact the lives of so many people, almost all of them I never would have been able to touch *without a book.*

You, like me, might be as business-minded as the next person and can already see how having a book will massively increase your bottom line. But I promise you the impact you have on the lives of others will be the most rewarding thing about having a book.

Have I piqued your interest? Aroused your curiosity and gotten your imagination going? Perhaps about how *your* book could impact your business, your life, and the lives of others? Good!

In fact, I am just the first of many professionals who will share why writing a book has changed their professional and, more often than not, personal lives. I'll share their stories and thoughts because if I were the only one who claimed writing a book was well worth the time, money, and energy, you might retain your not-yet-an-author status. But I'm not going to leave you hanging; in fact, I'm going to convince you (I'm sure of it!) that *You Must Write a Book*. And the sooner the better.

Yes, it is my intention to not only wipe out any remaining skepticism you have, but to inspire you to take immediate action *and* show you the way. There is a way to write a rock-solid book and have it professionally produced. That means even someone with the keenest eye wouldn't know a fancy traditional New York publisher didn't give you a big, fat advance and produce it for you. And, you can earn multiple (multiple people, multiple!) streams of income from it. Yes, even if you don't fancy yourself a writer—I sure didn't fancy myself to be one!

A tall order? Yes. Can I deliver? You bet.

The *original You Must Write a Book* was the 21st book I'd personally written, and, at the time, had more than a dozen on my "to write" list. Since then, I've crossed the fifty-book marker, and am continuing to write. I am (still) Hal Elrod's business partner in the Miracle Morning book series. As of this writing, we have published fourteen books in the series, with several more in the queue. Every year, I write and self-publish between three and six books and work with aspiring authors to help them craft, write, launch, publish, and market their books. Suffice it to say, I know a bit about successfully self-publishing business books. And I've written this particular book because I think you must write a book. If I hadn't written my first book, my business, heck my life, wouldn't be nearly as amazing as it is now ... and I want to give you the same, or even better, access to the opportunities that lie only on the other side of writing a book.

But you don't have to believe me. I'm not the only successful self-published business author. In fact, I know many people who have become household names, or at least very well known in their particular niches, because they first wrote and self-published their book.

Allow me to introduce you to Kevin Kruse.

I first heard about Kevin, an *Inc.* 500 serial entrepreneur and the *New York Times* best-selling author of *15 Secrets Successful People Know about Time Management*, when I saw a Facebook post about an "author's journey to $100K." In fact, the year Kevin published *15 Secrets,* his goal was to earn $100,000 as a full-time writer. He ended up earning a total of $242,042: $72,000 in royalties and just over $170,000 in speaking fees. Without his book, he wouldn't have gotten nearly as many speaking gigs, in fact, he probably wouldn't have gotten any at all because most of his speaking engagements arose from someone discovering his book.

Kevin shares his thoughts about writing a book:

Hardly a day goes by without someone asking me for advice on how to start a business or how to get their stalled business growing faster. I tell everyone the same thing: there is nothing more important than writing and publishing a book. I've started or cofounded several multimillion dollar companies, and I always start by writing a book for our target audience, which addresses their number one need. There's a reason why the root of "authority" is AUTHOR. The book will both generate leads for your business AND increase your close rate for the leads you already have. A book will be the best business card you'll ever have.

Find out more about Kevin at KevinKruse.com.

Kevin Tumlinson, author of *The 30-Day Author,* also weighed in:

Every professional would benefit from writing a book because having a book increases your credibility and authority on a topic. Beyond that, however, the process of writing a book allows you to develop a keener insight into yourself, your business, your industry, and your topic. Nothing helps you focus better than crystalizing your thoughts on the page in as concise a way as possible. Books can actually help you define the indefinable in your business and your life.

This Kevin can be found at KevinTumlinson.com.

My friends Richard Fenton and Andrea Waltz are the authors of several business parables including the best seller, *Go for No! Yes is the Destination, No is How You Get There.*

Here's what they said when I asked them why writing a book is a great idea for all business people:

It's our belief that everyone has a book inside them. However, most people think that they have to be the "definitive expert" of their topic or field. When you write a book, it's almost the exact opposite; you are sharing your current expertise with the reader and, in doing so, solidifying your credibility and expertise. This is not to say you don't need to have your facts down. But you don't have to be Julia Child to write a cookbook. You have your own style and way of doing things—to quote an American Idol phrase, "you make it your own."

Connect with Rich and Andrea at GoforNo.com.

Hal Elrod, my good friend, business partner, and author of a worldwide bestseller, says this:

Though I had many dreams of what I wanted to be when I grew up, "author" was never one of them. That is, until a close friend passionately said to me, "You have a responsibility to the world to share your process in a way that helps other people. The Miracle Morning transformed your life, so to keep it to yourself would be selfish."

Huh, I had never thought of it that way. So, I began writing. Slowly but surely (three years later), The Miracle Morning was finished, self-published, and on its way to becoming an international best seller and one of the highest rated books on all of Amazon.

*Writing and self-publishing The Miracle Morning is hands down, without question, the best decision I have ever made, for me and for my family. I believe that, for any author, the two most compelling reasons to write a book are to increase your **income** and elevate your **impact**.*

*In terms of **income**, becoming an author enabled me to double my speaking fees, triple my coaching fees, start putting on live events, launch a mastermind, and has created a seven-figure income stream from book royalties alone, all of which gives me the opportunity to provide financial security for my family. There is nothing else that gives me more peace of mind than knowing that I have the means to take care of them.*

*In terms of **impact**, The Miracle Morning has had an impact in the lives over 200,000 individuals around the world, and is* *increasing every day. By giving people a simple process that enables them to continuously grow and improve, it accelerates how quickly they are able to fulfill their potential and reach their goals. Nothing provides more fulfillment than knowing that the book is making a profound impact for nearly every person who reads it and that it will continue to do so long after I'm gone.*

There are hundreds, if not thousands, of other professionals who have taken on the challenge of self-publishing their first book and reaped the benefits of that decision. You can be next!

If you're wondering, and you probably are, whether you can, and should, write a book, you already know my answer. Turn the page, and I'll tell you why the *who is you!*

— 2 —
WHO MUST WRITE A BOOK?

Don't try to figure out what other people want to hear from you; figure out what you have to say. It's the one and only thing you have to offer.
—BARBARA KINGSOLVER

You might have all sorts of excuses rolling around in your head right now about why you must *not* write a book, such as *I am not a writer*, or *what would I possibly have to say?* Or even, *I don't have the time*. I can relate because I had all those thoughts and doubts rolling around in my head, too, before I wrote *Tall Order!*

While we aren't having an actual conversation, I can almost read your mind. I've convinced several of my friends and clients to write books, which means I've heard every excuse imaginable. I'll address the ones I mentioned above, a few others for good measure, and we'll go from there, okay?

I AM NOT A WRITER.

Au contraire, mon amie. You are a writer! You write every day. Notes, emails, briefs, text messages, Facebook posts, and assorted other documents—thousands of words a day, in fact, and you write them as easily as you breathe (this is important to note for later, so stay with me). If you can speak, you can write. If you can write, you can write a book. Writing a book is all about how you frame writing a book in your mind.

I recently had dinner with Zoe Galvez and Betsy Crouch from ImprovHQ. We were talking about their upcoming book and another book project they had contributed to recently. They were given twenty-two pages for their chapter, which seemed like an overwhelming number. Every time they sat down to write, their piece of the book felt *so big*. A book felt too big, too daunting, so they procrastinated, and kept putting it off. It wasn't until they gave the project a nickname, "Chappy," that the words started to pour out of them. Writing "Chappy" felt easy, like something they could do, because writing a small amount and on a topic they knew seemed simple. Ultimately, because they reframed what the project meant to them mentally, they were able to write with ease.

It is true that writing is a skill, and the more of it you do, the better you will get, and frankly, the easier it will become. I want you to keep in mind all writers start from the same place. Jump in with abandon and know that you will have a team to ensure your book turns out great.

There are tons of books on the writing craft, as well as many resources available to help you write better, write faster, and even write without moving your fingers, such as Dragon Dictate. While you will have a team to make your book read and sound amazing, you might want to become a better writer (which can be helpful in all areas of business writing), and there's no better opportunity to sharpen those skills than when you are embarking on the journey of writing a book.

I suggest you read these books to help you on your way. *You are a Writer* by Jeff Goins, *5,000 Words Per Hour: Write Faster, Write Smarter* by Chris Fox, and *30-Day Author* by Kevin Tumlinson.

WHAT WOULD I POSSIBLY HAVE TO SAY?

It is common for anyone to wonder what they could say that hasn't already been said. My answer is, *so, so much!* Your unique combination of life experience, education, and knowledge give you a unique voice and perspective. Putting this perspective and expertise in a book allows you to share your exclusive viewpoint with others, an unlimited number of others, in fact. Some of them you know, some you will meet as a result of your book, and some you may never know but whose lives you will enrich through your book.

You know more than you think and have much more to say than it might appear at first glance. I didn't know what I had to offer when Mark Victor Hansen suggested I write a book. *I can't come up with quite enough to fill an entire book.* Mark Victor Hansen asked if I had a popular presentation, a talk or speech I had been asked to give over and over again. Actually, I did, and he suggested I use that as the basis for my book.

When I was five years old, my dad ran a marathon in our hometown. I remember that he trained for months, would come home from running in the rain with wet clothing, go on runs with our family friend, John "the Wiz" Withers, and eventually he took third place in the race. As I got older, I would "go for runs" with him. We lived in a rural area, and as he got started on the old country road in front of our house, I would go with him. I ran for as long as I could, and when I petered out (in the beginning, after only about 200 yards), I'd sit on the side of the road and wait for him to come back by me on the way to the finish line (i.e., "home"). I would race him there and then declare myself the winner (never mind the fact that he had just run six more miles than I had).

The running bug bit me, and when my dad entered me in the 1977 Bonne Bell 10K in Cleveland (which was a big deal because Cleveland was about a zillion-hour drive from where we lived in Southeastern Ohio), I couldn't wait! I trained for months, and as soon as I finished and got my medal, I was hooked! I begged my parents for the next couple of years to let me run a marathon. Finally, when I was eight, my parents granted permission for me to train for and run the Athens Marathon. Nope, not the cool one in Greece ... still in Ohio, folks, *still in Ohio*. But a marathon, nonetheless, and I was not to be stopped! I ran every day after school and did my LSDs (not the drug; LSD in running speak means Long Slow Distance) on the weekends.

By the time I ran the marathon in April 1980, I had a few dozen races under my belt. The race organizer had contacted my dad after I submitted my application, and after being reassured I was fully prepared to not only run 26 miles and 385 yards, but to potentially do it in record time, they had a silver bowl made (just in case).

It was a rainy day, and honestly, all these years later, I really remember only two things: finishing and feeling worn out and excited at the same time and receiving my silver bowl at the awards ceremony afterwards (Well, three things. I promptly threw up in it after my mother gave me a Coke to rejuvenate my blood sugar ... which as it turns out, was not the best idea.)

Discovering my passion for running taught me many valuable lessons and set me up for success with my writing career. I learned planning, goal setting, and discipline. Although not many nine-year-olds would write a book, even then, in my relatively short time as a runner, that one race would have given me enough content to fill an entire book.

I believe it's never too early to think about what you can write a book about and begin the process.

HOW DO I BEGIN?

The original version of *Tall Order!* was a talk titled *Master Strategies for Explosive Business Growth*. I had given this talk about a dozen times to different audiences, and it helped me engage new clients and earned me additional speaking engagements. To convert this talk to a book, my first task was to memorialize it in writing. I sat down and "wrote my talk." It took about twenty hours to accomplish that task, and then I spent another couple of months filling in gaps, adding details and stories, and closing open loops.

I found turning my speech into written form was easy and at the same time difficult. Without the benefit of Dragon Dictate, or any other speech-to-text software that exists today, it took quite a while to capture it in writing. The easy part was writing what I knew; the difficult part was not losing my place, or forgetting an important piece, *losing my place*, or coming to the end of my available time to write while I was in a flow state.

I found that I don't tend to write and speak in exactly the same way, and you might discover the same thing. For example, it is easier for someone to follow along when we are talking, because they can interrupt, ask questions, and observe our facial expressions and body language. Also, we can go off on a tangent and still be understood because we can tell if the audience is keeping up.

If I wander off topic in a book and start talking about 1976 and how I was on a plane headed for vacation, I can't tell if you get my meaning and you would not only be confused, you would probably stop reading.

The point is, there are different considerations for speaking and writing, and you can learn what those are and how to apply them, just as you've gained other knowledge and skills for your business. If you have advice you've given over and over, which I'm certain you do, then you can use the strategy of getting it all out on paper first and then spend time organizing it in a fashion that makes sense in your book.

I Knew Enough to Fill a Book, and You Do, Too

If you're still relatively new to your profession, with five or fewer years of experience, or even if you are a new college graduate, I *still* believe you must write a book. Stay with me here. You have a tremendous opportunity to write your *first* book early in your career. I suggest you take one topic you find most interesting, or something you feel is important for others to know, and turn that into a book. Combine the knowledge you already have with research (reading books, talking to other experts, examples from clients), and you most definitely will have enough material to turn into a book. Alternatively, you might choose to first create a small ebook. I have several *Mini ebooks of...* in my catalog. Some topics can be covered well in seven to ten or even fifteen thousand words. You can have those printed in mini book formats, too, and they can very nicely replace your business card.

Many of the most popular books published today are short books that are quick reads. They go deep into one subject, solve one problem, and are easily digested by the reader.

You may be surprised by the power of your written words and whom they will reach. Ultimately writing books is all about positively touching and impacting other human beings, and there's no other feeling like knowing you've done that.

At a conference I attended, several people came up to share passages they had read in my book that gave them courage, inspired them to take action, or got them to think differently. This isn't about what my words had done, but I can think of no better way to convince you: My books create a connection between the readers and me. A business card simply can't do this for you. If I left this Earth today, I would go with a lot of inspiring words left behind for others, and that is a great feeling. I want that same great feeling for you as well.

Every single person, and I promise I'm not exaggerating, asks me the same question, "Coach, what would I possibly have to say that other people don't already know?" While our experiences carry threads of similarity, each individual has a unique perspective. What seems like "common knowledge" to you is definitely not to someone else. In fact, they are probably searching at this moment for the exact advice you have to share right now. Turn "giving advice to one person" into "sharing your book with many" and perhaps that will help you to realize a book is just another way to share some of the vast knowledge you have in you.

Here's the fun part for me, and I hope eventually for you, too: once I show people how it is possible for them to write a book and they do it, they want to write more books! I haven't met anyone who writes one book and then says, "No more, I'm done." I'm sure some of those people exist, I just don't know them.

You have within you enough valuable knowledge and a keen perspective to fill an entire book. That book can, and will, change your life and the lives it touches in one or a multitude of ways.

I DON'T HAVE THE TIME.

You probably don't have the time to write a book any more than you have time to read this one. I don't *have* time, either. Nobody has extra time where they have nothing to do. Everything you do starts with the decision that something is important enough to do, and then they carve out the time to do it.

I know single moms who work full time, raise their kids, and still find time to get a college degree. I know college students who take 21 credit hours, work two part-time jobs, and still find time to train for a 5K.

We all have the same 24 hours in a day, and you can use lack of time (or any number of equally ridiculous excuses) for not getting your book written. However, if you visit Chapter Five where I talk about how you can squeeze in writing your book, or even pick up a copy of my book *The Nifty 15: How to Write Your Book in 15 Minutes a Day* (The Prosperous Writers Book Series), you'll realize you absolutely can find the time to write your book. You know what else? You can start tomorrow (or even today).

Still wavering?

CONSIDER THE CONSEQUENCES

What are the consequences of not writing your book? Who will miss out on the knowledge you possess that could truly benefit? How many lives will you forgo helping if you don't make the time? If you do not tell your story, share your experiences, and make your knowledge available, no one else will. No one else can. It will be the world's loss, not just yours!

So, how do you know if you're the *who* I'm talking about? Hint: if you're reading this book, the *who* is definitely *you*!

Without question, and without meeting you personally, if you are a professional, I know you must write a book. But that's too simple of an answer, right? And if that were all I had to say, this would be a fifteen-page book, worthless to both of us. I'm not going to leave it there because if you have already gotten my point, you might have already started a Microsoft Word or Evernote document and begun to write your book. Even if you just started your interior design, financial planning, or estate planning practice in the last year or two, a book would still be an amazing addition to your toolbox (and a great replacement for your business card).

Although some might argue the point, even a neophyte has a valuable (albeit it fresh) perspective. Whether you happen to have more than 10 or even 20 years of experience, a book will persuade the unconvinced that *you* are the professional of choice, as opposed to the other guy who is saying the exact same thing you are.

A book says, *I am the expert here* unlike anything else.

If you are the unconvinced in this scenario, and you just might be, ask yourself these questions:

- Do I find myself giving the same advice over and over?
- When someone has a problem in my area of knowledge, are they asking me to help them solve it?
- Do lots of people have a problem or problems you can solve with your knowledge, experience, and education?
- Do you want to stand out from the crowd, generate more business, and make more money?

If the answer to the above questions, even for the most part, is yes, then guess what, sparky? *You must write a book.*

– 3 –
WHY WRITE A BOOK?

Writing a book opens doors much faster than a packet of information, a full presentation or proposal, or even pages of credible information and statistics.
—KEVIN TUMLINSON

We're rolling right along, and I've gotten you at least a little convinced a book is in your future. But you might think there are alternatives equally as effective and impressive. *Do I really have to go to all of the effort to write an entire book? Why, exactly, a book? Why not start a blog? Rock out a weekly podcast? Or do a newsletter?*

Sure, you could do any, or all, of those, but none of them have quite the same gravitas of a book. I still hold the conviction that you must *also* write a book. Here's why:

A BOOK IS THE HIGHEST FORM OF AWESOMENESS.

Yes, seriously, the average person who meets an author says, "Wow! You wrote a book? I've always wanted to do that. That's so cool!" Blogs, podcasts, and newsletters or even television appearances do not have the same prestige or command the same level of respect that a book does. None of them even come close to the same level of *wow* factor.

Want to dominate your market? Differentiate yourself from "that guy who says he does what you do" (but really doesn't)? Be the coolest of the cool at cocktail parties?

Have a book to hand out, and you will stand out.

A BOOK LIVES FOREVER.

It has been fifteen years since I published my first book. There are billions of people who haven't read it (yet), but they haven't missed their chance. Once you publish a book, it will be available for decades to come. In fact, here's something cool you might not know: your book can live forever *and* it can and will generate royalties for you and your estate (or heirs) for the rest of your life and 70 years after you die. How about them apples?

I even took that first book and revised, updated, and expanded it then re-released the 10th anniversary edition. This is the revised, updated, and expanded second edition of this book.

Author's Note: I thought a 10th anniversary edition of my book was cool until I saw the 50th anniversary edition of *You Learn by Living* written by Eleanor Roosevelt. Oh well, my day will come ... *Smile.*

Sooner or later, your business cards and brochures will become a piece of trash, yet I haven't found one person who would actually throw away a book. They will keep your book as a treasured possession and reference. Or, it will be passed on with high praise and a strong recommendation. It might even be donated so it can find its next right and perfect reader.

A BOOK ESTABLISHES AUTHORITY.

Your degree, certification, or licenses required many years combined with hard work to obtain, and although quite impressive, don't quite reach the same level of prestige as a book. Having a book with your name on it rises above anything else you can do because, in today's culture, a book is the ultimate proof you are an authority.

Authors are considered experts simply because they have a book. They get hired more often, more easily, and for more money. Being an author produces instant authority because a book solidifies your brand, establishes the highest level of credibility, and ultimately puts you head and shoulders above your so-called competition.

Said another way, a book is your opportunity to share your unique expertise. Don't make the mistake of taking your knowledge, experience, and education for granted. Just because what you know is second nature to you doesn't mean everyone (or even anyone) else knows what you know. And people are willing to pay you for what you know, especially if you can solve a problem, entertain them, or both. They will read your book and benefit from it alone, or they will recognize what a genius you are and hire you straight away (for higher fees than your colleague with no book, I might add).

A BOOK DIFFERENTIATES YOU FROM THE CROWD.

James Altucher, best-selling author of *Choose Yourself*, says, "If you've just given someone your business card, you've failed. I say, when you give someone your business book, you're about to impact someone's life and possibly make some money." In a world where many people seem to do what you do and know what you know, differentiation is key, and that key comes in the form of your book. Only a tiny fraction of your competitors have a book. Replacing your business card with a book provides a distinct advantage to your USP (unique selling proposition).

Sometimes, without having read the book at all, a client will hire you. Handing someone your book (and always offering to sign it) can be enough to cause a prospective client to pull the trigger and sign on the dotted line. It is true: just *having* a book is sometimes all it takes.

A BOOK HAS UNLIMITED REACH AND ALLOWS YOU TO EXPAND YOUR MARKET.

Your book will travel to places you cannot go, reach people you otherwise could not reach, and prepare prospective clients and customers for working with you and everything you have to offer.

Because you can make your book available online through Amazon, iBooks, and Kobo, (among a half-dozen other worldwide sales platforms), a book has a discoverability factor unlike any other sales tool. Not even your website can gain the visibility a book on one of the major sites can provide because *everyone* has a website (but not everyone, as you know, has a book).

You can't be in multiple places at one time convincing a future client of your brilliance, *yet that is exactly what your book can, and will, do.*

Cool, right? I can sense you are well on your way to being convinced (if you're not convinced already). But I'm not done. There's more! I have saved some of my favorite aspects and outcomes that result from writing and self-publishing a book for last.

A BOOK CAN BE REPURPOSED TO BECOME YOUR WHEEL OF FORTUNE.

Your $20 book can be repurposed or expanded into multiple streams of income, something I refer to as the Wheel of Fortune. A book can become an ebook, audiobook, workbook, seminar, coaching session or program, consulting gig, online course, keynote presentation ... and so much more. Repurposing and reusing the content of your book means multiple streams of income for your business. Combining a book with other offerings only serves to raise your overall profile and perceived expert status.

You remember Richard Fenton and Andrea Waltz, authors of *Go for No! Yes is the Destination No is How You Get There* from chapter 1. When I asked what having a book has done for them, they said this:

Deciding to write a book when we launched our speaking and training business was the smartest thing we ever did. First, we thought it could be a potential income stream, and it eventually was. But even more important, it was the fastest way we knew of becoming trusted experts in our field. We considered our book to be an educational business card. Having a book made selling our other products and services much easier. Our marketing message became a bit like this: If you like the book, you'd love to have us speak at your annual conference. *And it worked. We could have printed a four-color, six-page, glossy brochure, but nothing helps people understand your message better than your book will. And how much credibility does a brochure give you? Exactly.*

When you contemplate which topic you want to tackle in your book, think about it from the 30,000-foot perspective: what can you write about that you can also speak about, coach about, or expand upon in another medium? A book about the basics of crafting an estate plan can help you sell keynote presentations on the same topic. A keynote presentation about how to protect yourself in business with a limited liability corporation (or an S-Corp) can help you sell books and services on the same topic.

A BOOK CREATES BUZZ, AND BUZZ IS MANDATORY FOR YOUR SUCCESS.

Have you ever heard the marketing axiom, *it takes seven times for someone to recognize a brand*? Actually, in today's digital age, I think that number is substantially, perhaps exponentially, higher. While I'm surfing the net, I'm watching television, checking out Facebook and Instagram on my phone, and perhaps even fielding a call or two. Information, and advertisements, are coming at us at an astounding rate. I might notice some, or even a lot, but I'm missing *so much*. And I'm paying attention!

We are alike, you and me, so what are you missing because those that are marketing to you just can't get on your radar? More to the point, what are your potential prospects missing because you don't yet have a book? They won't miss your book, in fact, a book will cause most to stop and take notice.

A book can help start a buzz. A book makes it easy to spread your knowledge by word of mouth, and third-party validation is perhaps the strongest form of marketing. Buzz, word of mouth, and third-party validation are all key to your professional success.

A BOOK MAKES YOU [LOOK LIKE] THE ULTIMATE PROFESSIONAL.

The business person who appears to be the most professional, wins.

You have a book, you win.

What Do You Want from Your Book?

I would be remiss if I didn't stop for a second and ask you to examine what you want from your book. Obviously, you want to sell some books, get some new clients, and make additional income. That's your vision. But, what do you want specifically?

Setting goals for your book and then measuring your actions as well as your outcome will provide key data. You can use this data to predetermine your action plan and subsequent actions as well as analyze how your business and income have grown from having a book.

Before you ever write a word, you must determine "What's in it for me?" In other words, you must begin with the end in mind. Define what you want from your book—your vision, and then you can set specific goals. With your vision and goals to guide you, you'll make the best decisions about your book going forward.

There are different perspectives from which you can set goals for your book. The goals you set will inform and influence how you launch and market your book. You might want to make lots of money directly from sales. Perhaps you couldn't care less about selling your book, and you truly desire more clients or customers. Or, you might want book sales, more on-going business through clients and customers, and speaking gigs.

Take a moment to think through what you want from your book. When I'm daydreaming about what I want, I always start with a wish or two, *Wouldn't it be nice if "x" happened?* Wouldn't it be nice if I made as much money from this book as I do from serving clients? Wouldn't it be nice if my book was a #1 best seller in its category on Amazon for two years straight? Wouldn't it be nice if a new client hired me after reading my book? I marinate on the possibilities and really connect with what I want to happen from my book.

Then, I get more specific. I turn my wish into my want, *What I want from my book is ...* What I want from this book is an additional $1,000 or $10,000 a month in book sales income. Or, what I want from this book is $25,000 or $250,000 in new client revenue.

Your actions will be predicated upon your goals. Selling lots of books requires a slightly different set of actions than getting new clients from directly sharing your books with prospective clients. More on selling lots of books in chapter 10.

Identify a few tentative goals you have for your book. When you put together your plan of action, you'll have the opportunity to set more specific goals.

Tony Robbins, who came into the world's general consciousness through his book, *Awaken the Giant Within* (as well as through about a zillion infomercials for his Personal Power audio program), is widely known for saying, "If you develop the absolute sense of certainty that powerful beliefs provide, then you can get yourself to accomplish virtually anything, including those things that other people are certain are impossible."

I want you to be certain that you must write a book because when you must do something, objections and obstacles fall away. You will find reasons to write instead of procrastinating or avoiding writing altogether. As you tell others you are writing a book, they will encourage you to finish it and release it to the world.

It's Time!

I really wanted to ensure that by the time we dove together into the *how* of writing a book, you were clear about the importance of writing a book. When you have a strong enough *why*, you are far more likely to turn *I should write a book* into ***I must write my book***. Does that make sense?

When you are in the place where you know you must write a book, let's continue with the *how*.

— 4 —
Pre-Book Strategic Thinking: Before You Write Your Book

"Writing a book is the best thing you can do for your career and your bottom line."
—Honorée Corder

Before you can write even word *numero uno*, it is important to take a step back and a strategic app-roach to your book. It is critically important to determine what you want from your book, and the answer to that might mean you have to discover whether there's even a market for your book.

As we discussed in the previous chapter, a business book comes with almost unlimited opportunities. Your book can virtually replace your business card as you give it to prospective clients. You can sell it online through major retailers. You can use it as a lead generation tool in dozens of ways. Used properly, your book can be used to significantly grow your business and your income. Let's go a layer deeper about what specifically you want from your book.

Where to sell your book is a strategic decision based upon what you actually want from your book. Said another way, *what do you want from your book? What are your goals, and how will a book support your goals … and what specific goals do you then have for your book?*

Do you want better brand recognition? Do you want more clients or customers? Do you want to use a book as a door opener to speaking engagements or high-fee consulting? Do you want to sell lots of books and make money from book sales? Do you want to become the go-to expert in your field?

Or all of the above and more?

Writing a great book to use as a lead generator for your business is a fantastic goal. You can write and publish your book, become an author, and immediately begin using it to generate new business and income.

You have the additional option of publishing your book on Amazon and other major retailers to expand your reach, turning some of the content into a keynote speech or training session, and so much more.

Take a moment and write down some preliminary goals. You can finalize or "ink" them when you craft your plan.

The Wheel of Fortune

Selling your book in multiple formats and in multiple ways means you can create several additional streams of income from just one book.

Your book can definitely replace your business card and bring in new clients or customers to your business. You can make more money and attract more clients or customers than ever before with a paperback version of your book.

But you can also turn your book into multiple streams of income, not limited solely to multiple formats of the book, but also using the content of your book in multiple ways. I call the multiple streams of income the spokes on your Wheel of Fortune. As you can see below, there are many options to choose from, and you get to do just that: choose which among them might work for you.

Let's start with the book itself. Your paperback can be published as an ebook and audiobook. You can sell them on these platforms:

- Amazon Kindle
- Audible
- iTunes
- iBooks
- BarnesandNoble.com
- Kobo.com
- Draft2Digital
- And many others

If you stopped with multiple formats of your book, you could do quite well. But, and this is where I *get really excited* and want to light your fire, many other income streams can be derived from your books.

- **Keynote speeches.** Authors make more for presenting than those without a book. I personally know speakers, including Jeffrey Gitomer, Cameron Herold, and Hal Elrod, who command up to $50,000 *per speech*, and they are booked for these speaking engagements because someone loved their book. You can go from charging $1,500 or $5,000 to $10,000 or more once your book is published.

- **Online courses.** At a conference I attended earlier this year, one of the participants noted, "Right now, it's course-a-palooza." People who don't have time to read have the time to complete a course on the same content (while driving or exercising, for example), only a course costs more, sometimes significantly more (think $20 for a book, $200-$10,000 for a course). I would be remiss if I didn't mention the You Must Write a Book LIVE Coaching Course, you can find out more at HonoreeCorder.com/YouMust-Course.

- **A workbook, journal, or companion guide.** Most people learn better if there's a way for them to work through and apply the information being provided. You can repurpose the content of your book into a workbook people can buy once or multiple times. I created the *Prosperity for Writers Productivity Journal* when dozens of people requested a place to do the exercises I recommended in the original book. *The Miracle Morning for Salespeople* by Ryan Snow also has a companion guide that allows people to complete the exercises in the book.

- **Workshop or training.** Perhaps you're not a keynote speaker, but would love to conduct a full- or half-day workshop. Your book can be the basis for it, and you can charge hundreds or even thousands of dollars for admission.

- **Weekend events.** Hal Elrod hosts his Best Year Ever Blueprint event every December in San Diego to help people design their year, integrate the Life S.A.V.E.R.S. (his daily formula for success) into their mornings, as well as connect with like-minded people. Similarly, Tony Robbins turned his book, *Awaken the Giant Within* into a full weekend of transformation called Unleash the Power Within, complete with a firewalk and opportunities to purchase a considerable menu of other services, events, and merchandise.

- **Coaching.** My first book served to help me grow my one-on-one coaching business exponentially in the years following its publication. Not only did I personally sell tens of thousands of copies, I gave many away to prospective clients. Many who loved the book became clients, and some of worked with me for more than a decade. Now, some of those clients have published their own books as a result of a shift in our coaching focus.

- **Consulting.** You can offer high-level consulting, and you'll definitely engage more business with a book. Cameron Herold was the COO of 1-800-GotJunk? for six years, and now is an executive coach and consultant for Fortune 500 CEOs. He makes consulting fees for his expertise and also commands a revenue share for business he refers.

- **Mastermind.** Many authors who become known as one of *the* experts in their field offer private mastermind groups that can cost from a few thousand to tens of thousands of dollars and are by invitation only. I joined a mastermind two years ago to be in a room with the ability to ask questions and have them answered. Through that group, I have formed friendship and business alliances I would not been able to do any other way. As an expert, you can give limited access to a select group of individuals and be paid handsomely for it.

In two upcoming chapters, you will learn how to market your book *and* use your book to market your business. For now, jot down a few ideas you have to turn your book into multiple streams of income.

Before I continue, I have a special treat for you.

First Things First: Before You Write Your Book

I have asked my dear author friend Brian Meeks, a.k.a. the Vagabond Novelist, to write about a few other key things you will want to consider *before* you sit down to write.

I'll let Brian take it from here for a bit:
You've been thinking about writing a book. You've had a lifetime of experiences, been good at quite a few things, and even learned from the mistakes (we won't mention his name).

There are good reasons to become an author. Having a book lends credibility to speakers, it helps build a brand, and can even impress that annoying aunt who won't quit asking you when you're going to get married and start having children.

The first logical step is to see if your idea has been taken by someone else. You get on Amazon and find that the niche is greatly underserved. In fact, you don't really find anyone who has covered your area of expertise in much detail.

So, it's time to start writing, right?

Well, maybe. Actually, no. There are some questions to ask. The first one is, who is your book for?

If you answer "everyone," then you're not ready. In the book business, we refer to an avatar (which Honorée discusses in detail in chapter 5) when discussing the potential market for your book. An avatar is shorthand for the ideal person that would want to read your book and would pay to do so. (Author's Note: Your avatar may also double as an ideal client or customer.)

You might think that hydroponic gardening is the best thing in the world and that everybody should do it, but the hard-core video game crowd (as just one example) isn't going to be interested in your book. Neither are the traveling circus folks with a propensity for knitting. Who has time to garden when there are tents to set up and sweaters to make?

One needs to really consider an audience before spending the time and money to go through the entire book process. It's a lot of hours to invest only to find out that the book you intend to write, *Squirrel Training for the Professional Glockenspiel Enthusiasts*, won't be the runaway best seller you imagined.

The next question might be, how many professional musicians are there in the United States? (It's not quite time to start thinking about foreign rights deals.)

At any given time, there are 64,000 musical groups and artists in the US according to one site on the Internet. Another puts the number of professional singers at 240,000. Even if we add those together, we still get only 304,000 people, give or take, and how many of those play the Glockenspiel?

We don't need to know exactly how many play the Glockenspiel because we do know that some percentage of the group plays the guitar and some play the trombone, while others play the drums. Now, the latter group might also dabble in the glockenspiel, but certainly not all of them.

We might next ask, how many musicians play percussion instruments?

Let's say we assume that 10 percent of the musicians play a percussion instrument and that 100 percent of those people are either professional glockenspiel players or secretly want to be; that still leaves only 30,400 potential readers.

Now, 53 percent of all adults in the United States never read a book after they finish school regardless of whether they drop out of high school or get a PhD. That means that our group of potential readers, which we've made some wildly optimistic assumptions about, has just been narrowed to 14,288.

How many of those people want to learn how to train squirrels?

Again, because I'm feeling generous. Let's assume 97 percent because squirrels are freaking adorable. That's roughly 13,859 people.

If you sold your book to all of them at $4.99 on Amazon as a Kindle book with royalties currently at 70 percent, you'd make about $3.45 per sale. Your total take would be $47,814 dollars.

That would be great, but here's the rub. We've been unreasonably optimistic in our assessment of the audience, and it probably isn't a fraction of what we've come up with. And, even if divine intervention had led to an accurate audience number, how will you find them all?

Bottom line, you're going to sell twelve copies of your squirrel training book to friends and family members, and it's going to leave a bad taste in your mouth.

This isn't the end of the road, though, and there is good news.

Once you've realized that the dream book you'd like to write doesn't make financial sense, you can ask if there are other reasons to write it. Keynote speakers can make $5,000–$25,000 for a single speech, and maybe you have a sense of humor and can parlay your love of squirrel training via classical glockenspiel music into your own niche that could lead to other streams of income.

Also, maybe you go another route, and instead of trying to teach glockenspiel players to train squirrels, you write a book for women who want to train squirrels. There are lots of women in the US.

The point is, one can quickly determine if a book idea makes sense with a few searches on Google and asking the right questions.

Now, get out there and figure out what sort of rodent-related book you'd like to write. I know you can do it.

Brian makes many excellent points, and hopefully in a way that caused you to think while you were laughing hysterically. Let me boil down what Brian and I are trying to help you accomplish: we want you to do an assessment of the true market for your book and determine whether a large enough market exists for you to write the book or alternatively whether there are other reasons to justify the time and expense. While having a book might not result in lots of book sales, it could be the catalyst for helping you earn lots of income in other ways.

Book Reader Facts

If you desire to make multiple streams of income from your book and not use it as a way to find new business exclusively, there are several considerations to keep in mind.

About 70 percent of American adults have read a book (in whole or in part) within the past year. Men are more likely to read nonfiction books than fiction, while the opposite holds true for women: the majority of women read fiction, and almost half also read nonfiction, (NEA Report, 2013).

Women read more (between five and fourteen books per year) than men (between three and nine), and people with a higher education tend to read more than those with less education. The typical college graduate or someone with an advanced degree reads an average of 17 books each year, compared with nine for high school grads and three for those who did not graduate from high school.

Here is some good news: young adults (those between the ages of 18 and 29) are more likely than their elders to have read a book in the past 12 months. Eighty percent of young adults read at least one book, compared with 71 percent of those ages 30 to 49, 68 percent of those 50 to 64, and 69 percent of those 65 and older. Younger people are reading books, whether they are physical books, ebooks on their phone or other digital device, or even consuming them in audio form.

Recently, a mortgage broker who wanted to write a book for other mortgage brokers contacted me. An analysis of mortgage brokers, combined with the above statistics and Brian's way of analyzing a market, was quite revealing.

The majority of mortgage brokers are men between the ages of 35 and 55, with at least a high school education (it is unknown what percentage of them have college degrees), making them unlikely to buy and read his book. In addition, there are only 400,000 mortgage brokers total in the US, which means that *even if* 10 percent of them were to find out about his book and read it, he certainly couldn't parlay the sales of 40,000 books into a living. At $15 per book, total sales would equal $600,000, or the equivalent of about three years of mortgage broker income. The net profit would be a fraction of this total, making the end certainly not justify the means.

We suggested he pivot his focus and write a book for real estate agents, a market of about two million, which is predominantly women. Writing a book targeted at real estate agents gave him a greater chance of making several streams of income from the book itself, as well as drive referral business to him through some of those same Realtors.

Having a book designed with forethought and written with intention and purpose will increase his main mortgage business income, as well as provide perhaps a dozen other streams of income. It will even act as a recruiting tool because he can pass it out to mortgage brokers not yet on his team as a way to convey his processes and personality.

A book can do the same for you, too. Are you excited yet? Because I sure am!

Once you have come to the conclusion that writing your book is, indeed, the right decision for you, it's time to answer yet another question, *how is the book going to get written?*

— 5 —
HOW TO WRITE YOUR BOOK

*When you're committed to writing your book,
you will find a way to write it.*
—HONORÉE CORDER

If you're like me, once you're convinced to do something, you want the 1-2-3 on how to get it done in the fastest, most efficient, and best way ... and you want to get started *right now*.

I'm not going to waste even a single moment of your time. This chapter covers *how* you must write your book, and in the next chapter, the options available to you to actually get the book produced.

QUALITY IS PARAMOUNT

I learned critical self-publishing lessons the hard way. A book with mistakes or a crappy cover will not only be a disservice to you, it will cause people to dismiss your book and you as well. A well-crafted book can do so much for your business, brand, and career. A book that is poorly done can backfire, doing more harm than good. I wouldn't want your book to do the exact opposite of what you intend for it to do, and I know you don't either.

I remember when my friend Jeffrey Gitomer, whom I met after I used a quote of his in my first book, said, "Honorée, your writing is really good. This book looks like shit." Always one to be direct, he didn't pull any punches or try to soften his true opinion to save my feelings.

To this day, I am grateful for his insights and advice. I chose not to curl up in the fetal position, but to take his mentorship and suggestions to heart. I got the cover re-done and put some of the same finishing touches on the book I'm going to suggest to you. I even changed the title, because yes, even the title was *awful*. I do believe I burned all remaining copies of that original book, so I can't produce a copy to show you a before and after (thank goodness!).

When I see a book with a lousy cover, I want to hug the author because I know the hours of work that went into writing it, only for them to publish one that doesn't represent all their effort. Please do not cut corners by settling for a horrible cover or rush to get the book out before it is ready and, in the process, fail to have it properly designed, edited, and proofread.

The goal is to publish a book that is indistinguishable from traditional publishing.

Make sure you read that sentence again. This is what it means: When someone holds your book in their hands, it needs to have the look, feel, and read of a New York traditionally published book.

James Altucher had this to say about self-publishing:

I professionally self-published what I now call Publishing 3.0 *by engaging the best cover designer, editor, and copywriter, and then wrote a solid marketing plan, did a podcast tour, spoke at conferences, and encouraged word of mouth until it became a best seller. It's three years later, almost to the day, and it's still selling. Quality publishing is key to success and book sales.*

How do you make that happen? Have your book edited, proofread, designed (have a fantastic cover and get it carefully formatted), the sales copy written by a top-shelf copywriter, and ultimately, it can be published professionally.

To accomplish this seemingly overwhelming feat, first I want you to recognize it is possible. It is done every single day and can be a relatively simple process. Keep reading, and, as suggested, take the actions necessary to make it possible for *your book*. I'm right here with you, guiding you each step of the way.

Very simply, your action steps are to

- weigh your options,
- get yourself organized, and
- get down to the business of writing your book.

OPTIONS FOR WRITING THE BOOK

You have several options when it comes to actually writing the book. Here are two:

- **Write it yourself.** I recommend this option if you are a writer, are comfortable with writing, do a lot of writing anyway, or are up for the challenge. Investment cost: *free*. Well, sort of. The cost of your time, which I consider most precious, won't necessarily require an out-of-pocket investment. Only you can decide if you want to take on the challenge of doing it yourself.

I personally love writing books (obviously), but while I think you must write a book, I don't think you necessarily must do all the writing, so you can do either of the following, as well:

- **Hire a ghostwriter or content creation specialist.** A great ghostwriter can work with you to identify your message, craft the tone and contents of the book, and produce a final fantastic product. And, then there are folks who specialize turning your expertise into a book you can hold in your hands, as well as create post-publication content to drive sales and help you get more clients. This type of investment ($20,000-$100,000 or more), is a custom option that can yield multiple dividends. The ghostwriters and content specialists I recommend are authors and journalists themselves who know how to extract information, create a manuscript that will work hard on your behalf, and contain content that convert lookers into buyers. I have several top-shelf recommendations, and if you'd like one, email me personally at Honoree@HonoreeCorder.com.

Now that you know what the other options are, let's assume you're going to do the majority of the heavy lifting (i.e., the writing) yourself. Here are some key tips for *making* time to write your book and *how* to actually get it done in a reasonable amount of time.

Note: Even if you're going to engage one of the outsourcing options, above, you will still need to intentionally carve out a significant amount of time to complete your book. It won't magically appear on your desk one day; the process requires quite a number of time-consuming and critical steps that you must be involved in (and we haven't discussed the launch and marketing pieces of your book project yet). Do yourself a favor: read through these steps and the rest of this book so you will have a clear picture of what's to come.

Crafting Your Book

IDENTIFY WHAT PROBLEM YOU'RE GOING TO SOLVE AND/OR WHAT ADVICE YOU'RE GOING TO SHARE.

You know from experience and client interaction what advice your clients need most often. What are the most common problems you see? What do you find yourself repeating most often? What do you wish people would know, do, or not do? If they could just live in your head for one day, would you solve a problem they have, provide pleasure they don't know exists, or both?

Pull out a journal or a piece of paper and brainstorm some ideas. Like any professional, I'm sure you find yourself fielding some of the same questions on a regular basis. Additionally, if you're like me, you might have made a mistake or two (or 367!) you would prefer to have avoided; these are lessons you can pass along in print.

After writing and self-publishing 20 books and helping in the production of many others, I am constantly asked, should I write a book, and what's the best way to do it? This book is the answer to those questions. While I have several clients I'm coaching through the process, I can't coach everyone, and I'm passionate about two things: *One*, every professional would benefit from writing a book. And *two*, that book needs to be done professionally (or not at all).

I am certain after a short period of contemplation, you will easily identify at least one book idea you can test for validity, proof of concept, and commercial appeal. I'm sure you are passionate about a few things within your area of expertise, advice you would want everyone to have, and advice your future readers wish they had! I would have loved a book about when to do estate planning, or how to begin investing, or what the best tax planning strategies are … about twenty years ago.

A prospective reader (and client) would benefit from knowing right now the information and expertise you take for granted. While I'm focused on why writing a book is a great idea for *you*, equally as important is the help your book is going to provide your readers as a standalone or allow you to aid someone who might otherwise not have been able to find you.

Once you've crystallized which problem you want to solve (because there might be others, and therefore other books), write it down. Look at it a few times a day. Jot down the different aspects of the advice you want to provide. Allow your initial idea to morph and expand into what it will eventually become.

OBTAIN EFFECTIVE FEEDBACK.

You'll want to run it by a few people to see if they think it's a great idea. Whether the title has been identified or not, you'll want to be able to describe your book idea in a few sentences. You should be able to complete this sentence:

I'm writing a book for _____
about how they _____.

For example, *I'm writing a book for professionals about how they can successfully self-publish a book, improve their brand, increase their authority, and their platform.*

Or, *I'm writing a book for people who have been through a divorce and want to create a new life they love.*

When I hit upon the idea to write *You Must Write a Book*, I asked several of my former business coaching clients (the same folks I successfully convinced to write books), a publishing public relations expert, and several of the people I interviewed for this book. To a person, I was given a double thumbs up, a green light, and a few "Yes, please, I can't wait to read your book so I can finally write mine!" responses. One best-selling author was so excited about this book that he responded to my email request for an interview with an immediate phone call. I took all of this as a sign to start writing.

You might find, as did our mortgage broker, that despite having a great idea, he wasn't going to achieve his desired outcome from his original book idea. But the same content, shifted a few degrees, will increase his target market and, therefore, his chances of financial success.

Source Qualified Input

Your idea could have legs, and you can and should also gather other input that can make it even better. There are multiple resources you can consult to acquire confirmation for your ideas.

Successful Business Authors.

When asking for opinions about your book idea, be sure to consult those who know what they are talking about. Ask other business book authors about their experience with either generating new business or selling books. Make sure their books have been professionally published. For research purposes, it doesn't matter if they are traditionally or self-published. But, there's no sense taking advice from someone who just put any old cover on their book and "did everything for less than $300." A successful author whose books sell over the long term (as opposed to someone who had a

#1 Amazon best seller for about 10 minutes) is a great person to bounce an idea off of—no matter how they brought their book to market.

YOUR FAN CLUB (I.E., YOUR CLIENTS).

In addition, ask your clients what type of advice they'd love to have at their fingertips. Because they are already clients, you have their trust as well as their money. As fans of your work, I'm certain they would love a chance to tell you which expertise they'd love to have access to for the price of three cups of coffee. You can even conduct a poll or do a survey and include not only your current clients, but also past clients and other important connections.

THE 'ZON.

Do a search on Amazon for books related to your topic. The second largest search engine in the world puts a powerful tool at your fingertips … for free. In just a few minutes, you can find out if other books on your chosen topic exist (proof of concept!), give you a sense for what types of covers work for the best sellers in your category (ideas for your designer!), and even help you visualize how awesome it would be to see your book on that first search page!

A NOTE OF CAUTION.

I've seen people with barely any true business experience dole out legal advice (incorrect legal advice, I might add). Just as you wouldn't consult a kindergarten teacher for tax advice, you should test your book idea with those who have a line of sight into whether your idea truly holds water.

I have a client who has friends who are giving her publishing advice. They've never published a book and have no insight into what will or won't work, and yet they have no problem sharing their opinions. We both appreciate that their hearts are in the right place, but thankfully my client is wise enough to give the right amount of weight to her friends' advice.

Once you've picked a topic and decided how you want to tackle it, you'll want to …

CREATE AN OUTLINE.

Crafting your book will go more smoothly if you work from an outline. You'll write your desired daily word count and reach your goal of having a book, much more easily with an outline that's solid and thought out.

Before I started writing this book, I crafted a rough outline. Here's the actual initial outline for this book:

I. Why I wrote a book

II. Who should write a book

III. Why write an actual book

    a) Why not a blog or newsletter, etc.

IV. How to write

    a) Getting it written

    b) Publishing

V. Marketing the book

VI. Who else has successfully written and self-published a business book.

As you can see, that's a pretty rough outline and not much like the book looks today. I started with what I considered the easiest path to fleshing out an outline: using the w questions: who, what, where, when, and why … and of course, the how. I suggest, at least initially, you use a similar process to flesh out your outline.

- *Who* has the problem you can solve?
- *What* do they need to do to avoid pain or gain pleasure, or both (i.e., what is your advice for them)?
- *What* do they need to do, or avoid doing, to stay out of trouble, get out of trouble, or get the thing, event, or awesomeness they want?
- *Where* do they need to go, or avoid going, to get their desired result?
- *When* do they need to take action?
- *Why* must they do, or not do, what you're advising?
- And, finally, *how* do they get what they want, or avoid what they don't want?

This book, even as I write (and review) it, is still changing and expanding as I discuss it with my clients who are writing their books, my author friends, and even my editor. By the time you read these words, the final book will barely resemble the original outline. You can expect that your original idea will evolve into an expanded, even greater version, and this is a normal part of the process.

Once you have an initial outline, writing is going to be a breeze. Why do I say that? Because you're going to be writing about what you know!

Outline and then ...

After crafting an outline, take the time to also do the following:

Create an Avatar (a.k.a. ideal reader).

Brian referenced having an avatar in the previous chapter. Imagine you have your ideal, most favorite, and wonderful client or customer sitting in front of you. You are giving them the advice they have asked for … you don't have any problem doing that, right? Of course not, because (drum roll please) *you're the expert!* If I asked you a question about financial planning, or forming a new entity, or how you handled office politics back in the 80s, you wouldn't hesitate; you would simply speak. When you craft your avatar, keep in mind that in your book you are *giving advice to your favorite client.*

Before you start writing, list the qualities and characteristics of your ideal client. Describe the perfect person, couple, or company, whose custom would make you ecstatic. Use your very favorite client as an example. This will become your avatar. Here's an example, a short take on my ideal reader for this book. And yes, it's an actual person, one of my favorite clients:

<u>Eric Negron</u>

Financial Advisor, 10 years' experience

College educated, finance and economics degree

31 years of age

Married with three children

Homeowner

Mid-six-figure income, which he intends to multiple by three to four times

Accredited Wealth Management Advisor from College for Financial Planning

Focus: High Net-worth planning

Problem:

- wants to multiply his business
- not considered "grey" enough
- needs more credibility with ultra-wealthy investors

As I write about why you, my reader, should write and self-publish a book, I actually have Eric in mind. He's a long-time client and friend, and yes, we've had multiple conversations about why he should write a book. When you remember what your ideal client needs to hear, you will give targeted advice. My advice to Eric works perfectly as my advice to you and a wide range of other people. But an avatar focuses my thoughts. While your situation might be somewhat unique, 95 percent of the advice is applicable and is exactly what *you* need to write your book.

As a side note, I have a few other people in mind as well. But when it comes to giving actual advice, I think about what, in particular, I want to tell Eric. It helps me make decisions from content (Should I include this?) to the prose (Is this the best way to describe this concept?).

Get 'er done!

So, future author friend, by now you have your outline and your avatar. Now you need to ...

SCHEDULE TIME TO WRITE EVERY DAY.

Yup, every day. Or at least six days a week. Establishing a writing habit will help you to get the writing done and also build the muscles (and skills) you need to do the actual writing. As I mentioned earlier, I write every morning from 6:00–7:00 a.m.

Some days are easier than others, and yet I still sit and write (even if the words aren't that great or suck, or I end up scratching them completely at some point). I write no matter what. It will get easier; the more you write, the better you'll get, and the more you'll write (and want to write). I'll share more on this in Chapter Twelve.

If you want more tips for building a daily writing habit and Steve Scott's take on self-publishing, you might also want to read *The Miracle Morning for Writers*.

SET A PUBLICATION GOAL DATE.

Pull out your calendar and schedule a date to have your book published. If you've read any of my other books, you know I'm a fan of 100-day cycles, specifically completing a goal within 100 days. If you're interested in my philosophy on goal achievement, check out my book *Vision to Reality*.

Before your head explodes, keep in mind that your eventual book will contain approximately 40,000 words. Note: 10,000 words is the size of a pamphlet, 20,000 words equals a short ebook or print book, 40,000–50,000 words is a pretty good-sized nonfiction book (and about the size of all my nonfiction books). To accomplish writing a book, one day at a time, I suggest you …

SET A DAILY WORD COUNT GOAL.

Can you set a goal to write 400 words per day? Yes, you can because about ten minutes ago you wrote an email that probably had at least half that many words in it. You just didn't call it *writing*, so you weren't concerned about counting the number of words. "Oh my goodness, that email had 764 words in it. I had writer's block, and it took me three weeks to write it!" said no one, ever.

A book can sometimes feel much bigger than anything else, so psychology plays a role in how hard you might be making writing a book in your head. Right now I have three emails in my just-send outbox, the word count of each is 178, 212, and 398, respectively. I was able to compose them in minutes because I knew what I wanted to write, I entertained no doubts about my ability to do so, and I performed the physical act of writing. You could think of a book as just writing a couple of hundred emails. Cranking out several hundred words a day in the form of email over the course of 100 days (or even six months, which is 180 days) is easy like a Sunday morning. The words will flow from your fingertips like water over a dam. The same goes for writing your book. Four hundred words over 100 days is 40,000 words. One hundred and eighty days gives you either 72,000 words or 40,000 words in an actual published book (the extra 80 days is plenty of time to take the necessary steps to publish).

Since you're not going to be making anything up, you'll be able to easily capture your words. I think you'll be more like me than you think: I don't have a "what do I write" challenge, I have a "when am I scheduled to write" challenge!

I find I have to hold my writing time sacrosanct, and I do. It is pretty much inviolate—unless I'm sick or running to catch an airplane at the time I've scheduled, I write. You can, and must, too.

What Else, Coach?

While you're in the process of writing your book, there are some other action items to complete as well.

Form Your Book Team.

The team you need to self-publish your future income-earning business book is critical to your success. Fortunately for you, I have more than 50 books' worth of experience, and each book needed a quality team to produce the quality book. (For those of you doing the math in your head, this book was my 21st, since this book was first published, I've written thirty more, and I've helped produce fourteen in *The Miracle Morning* book series.)

As you'll see, I have team members you can hire for your own book. Or you can take my suggestions to find someone or use someone you know.

Here goes:

- **A book cover designer.** You (and everyone else) *so* judges a book by its cover. You need *the very best book cover you can get*. You'll pay between $300 and $2000 (or more) for a book cover that compels someone to read your book. Because you get only one chance to impress a prospective reader, do yourself a solid and spare no expense to get the best you can. You can visit HonoreeCorder.com/YouMustBonuses for my personal recommendations.

- **A top-notch editor.** An unedited book is one that actually *does* get thrown in the trash, or at least deleted or returned (I actually burned mine in my fireplace, true story).

    The kiss of death to a potential client in a business book is a typo, misspelled, or even missing word.[1] While no book is perfect, and no matter how many eyes you have on a book, something is bound to slip through, having an editor will create a smooth ride for the reader and work hard on your behalf to turn a prospect into a client.

    There are three basic types of editing: developmental, copyediting, and proofreading. A developmental or content edit helps you take your good book and make it great by ensuring you have all the necessary elements in the right order. A copyedit takes your great book and delivers the information in a smooth and clear way. The

---
[1] If you noticed a typo, misspelled, or missing word in this book, kindly email Assistant@HonoreeCorder.com so we can correct it right away!

proofread turns a smooth and clear great book into one that is also error free—or as near as may be. Your book may not need each level of editing, but you'll want to get a professional assessment.

Keep in mind that quality editors are in high demand, and you should seek to engage the editor of your choice about three months before you think you'll be ready. (Note: scheduling an editor will add an extra layer of accountability to your writing process. You're welcome.)

For information on my editing team, visit HonoreeCorder.com/YouMustBonuses. (My editor will offer you $50 off any project over $1000 if you mention this book when scheduling your time with Before & After Editing.)

- **A proofreader.** Once all edits and corrections have been made, hire a professional proofreader to give the manuscript one final look and catch any remaining mistakes. Of course my bench of excellent editors and proofreaders can provide this critical service, and you'll find them by visiting HonoreeCorder.com/YouMustBonuses.

  Note: You'll want to book your editor and proofreader at the same time. To determine when you'll need your proofreader, ask how long the editor will need to edit (this will depend upon your writing skill level, as well as the length of your book. Include how much time you'll need to work through your edits (it usually takes me a few days, you might need a week or two). Good proofreaders are also booked a month or more, so don't wait until you're ready to get on their calendar. If you do, you'll add unnecessary time to your production schedule.

- **An interior designer.** No, not the person who selects your lamps and throw pillows. I'm talking about someone skilled in making the interior of your book have the look and feel of a *New York Times* Best seller. The lead-time for formatting is three to six months, be sure to put formatting on your calendar and theirs as well. (For a current list of recommended formatters, please visit the Resources Page.)

- **A copywriter.** A copywriter composes the prose for the back cover of your book, and your retail sales page also known as sales copy. Writing sales copy, or copywriting, is a special skill and should be left to someone who has honed it. I consider myself a writer, but I do *not* consider myself a copywriter! I use two folks, both with more than twenty years of real-world book writing and publishing experience, and I'll share their names with you if you're really nice and tell me I'm smart. Or you can visit HonoreeCorder.com/YouMustBonuses, no compliments necessary.

THE POINT IS ...

You must write a book, and you must make the time to write it and hire the best team you can to take care of the tasks you can't. Right now, it's 7:04 a.m. on a Saturday morning. Everyone else in my house is sleeping (including the cats ... especially the cats!). I write from 6:00–7:00 a.m. every morning, six to seven days a week. More on this in Chapter Twelve, but here's what to keep in mind right now: *there's always a way to do something, when you commit to doing it.* Period.

Look my new friend, I'm a former business coach, and I still live in the world of *no excuses.* Your excuses won't hold water with me because I've heard them all, and what I know for sure is the moment you decide you are going to write and publish a book (or get a book written and published), you will.

My alarm went off at the same time it does every day, and you know what? Today I didn't wake up and say, "Woohoo! Another 1000 words, three book projects require immediate attention, and I get to do some laundry too!" I could've slept in and been damn happy about it. But I know, and you know too, that sleeping longer wouldn't allow me to insert a little humor and sarcasm into this book so you too can get your book written. Honorée sleeps in = lose-lose. Yet now that I'm up and writing, I'm loving it and feeling proud that I didn't let temptation win. I'm human, you're human, and I know you can do this. Okay? Okay.

I have tons of suggestions for when how to write, but here are the basics: pencil out a few times you could fit in writing, such as: before work, during your lunch break, or after the kids go to bed. Gather the support you need from the important people in your life. Put a recurring appointment on your calendar, and keep those appointments. Before you know it, your book will begin to take shape. You will love having the first copy of your book in your hot little hands. Hold that image in your mind, and begin.

You should, by now, have at least an idea percolating about the book you're going to write, an avatar in mind, a block of time when you will write every day, and the beginnings of your book team formed. Next, we'll cover the technical parts of self-publishing.

— 6 —

HOW YOU CAN SELF-PUBLISH YOUR BOOK

Self-publishing an amazing book is easier than ever. You just need to know what to do and what not to do.
—HONORÉE CORDER

Amazon has changed the lives of many authors, including mine, by introducing the Kindle and with it Kindle Direct Publishing (KDP), thereby opening up a channel to connect writers with readers. Amazon provides publishing of ebooks and print (both through KDP), and audiobooks (accessible through ACX.com) options.

I can honestly say, *I'm so grateful for Amazon.*

Other major companies have jumped on board, so you'll want to check out Apple's iBooks (https://www.Apple.com/iTunes), and Kobo, which is huge in Canada and actually distributes to over 190 countries all over the world (https://www.Kobo.com/WritingLife), as well as Draft2Digital (they distribute to all of the major online distribution channels, including libraries; https://www.Draft2Digital.com). There are others, but these are the main retail platforms, and where you'll want to start.

With the introduction of self-publishing, and the fact that professionally self-publishing a book is now not only possible but actually quite easy, I believe there is almost no reason to attempt traditional publishing.

Why Not Traditional Publishing?

I don't want to spend too much time on this subject, but I do feel it is worth a mention. For anyone who has held out the hope they can and might be chosen by a traditional publisher, I encourage you not to waste your time (with one caveat; wait for it, it's coming).

Much has been said about traditional publishing, and for me, it boils down to simple economics: unless and until I have the same opportunity to make the living I am accustomed to making now from my writing with traditional publishing, I choose self-publishing. I cannot command a million-dollar advance, even after selling a combined total of more than 1.6 million books. More than fifty books, and one and a half million copies sold, and I still could not garner anything more than a meager advance. That is why I believe traditional publishing is not an ideal choice.

If, however, you aren't interested in making money from your book, and you simply want a book and the caché that comes with a traditional publisher, go for it.

The Caveat: *If you can obtain a seven-figure advance, free and clear or with incredible terms, for your book, then I say,* **Go for it!** *With few exceptions, I ardently believe you will be well served to publish it yourself.*

Great News!

Self-publishing is the remaining and best choice for the vast majority of people. Which in and of itself is, and I say this without any reservation, *an incredible opportunity.*

Without the ability to self-publish a professional book, you'd be left to establish your credibility and build your business one meeting, one business card, and one day at a time. But you aren't—the one option you have is, in my opinion, the very best option!

I am so grateful I discovered and took advantage of the option to self-publish. I started this journey at a time when it still had a distinct and unpleasant odor. Believe me, in 2004 and 2005 when I was self-publishing and selling lots of copies, some people still turned up their noses at me when they discovered I had *self-published*. Today, friends of mine who were traditionally published tell me that it wasn't quite the joy ride they expected it to be (and have since bought back their rights or are patiently waiting to do so).

In Chapter Nine, I share your options for distribution and marketing based on your overall business goals and of course, the goals you have for your book.

For sure, you want a book that, when someone holds it in their hands, *they are impressed.* They are impressed with you and what you know, your level of expertise. They feel strongly enough to consider what you have to offer, quite possibly, as the only way they can either solve a problem they have, or achieve an outcome they desire.

With that said, let's discuss a few of the finer points of self-publishing.

AND THEN: SELF-PUBLISHING THE BOOK

This is the technical portion of how to self-publish, the "what" you need to know to actually do it. This portion actually comes in two parts: First, things to consider and decide and, second, actions to take.

Section I: Things to Consider and Decide

While a book has several important components, there are a few that set the stage for a book's success. You must consider your options (*what makes a good title?*) and decide (*this is my title, price, etc.*), and strategy will inform and influence what you decide for each one. I'm going to cover each component here, and then in the next chapter, discuss the approach and strategy pieces as they pertain to you, your market, expertise, and desired outcomes. I've also provided a reference section in the back, including other books to read, websites to visit, and other goodness you'll want to check out.

Your Title

Like a well-designed book cover, a well-crafted title will grab a prospective reader by the shirt and compel them to read your book. You want your title to (a) say exactly what the book is about (*You Must*

Write a Book), (b) be incredibly memorable (*Save the Cat*, a book about writing a screenplay), (c) be very intriguing (*The Life Changing Magic of Tidying Up*), or (d) all of the above (such as *The 4-Hour Work Week*).

Here are some tips for crafting a fabulous title for your book:

KEEP IN MIND YOUR TITLE IS THE "WHAT."

What is the book about? This book is about why you must write a book. I read *Awaken the Giant Within* because I wanted to become the best version of myself. Read Gary Vaynerchuk's book, *Crush It*, if that's what you want to do. You can choose to follow a simple formula: The A's Guide to X, Y, and Z. Examples might include *The Professional Writer's Guide to Writing, Publishing, and Selling a Million Books* or *The Individual's Guide to Finding, Getting, and Spending Your Inheritance*. Or, you might want a more direct approach, such as *Write to Market*, Chris Fox's book about writing a book that will sell, which was the predecessor to *Launch to Market*, his book on how to launch the book to a desired target market. You'll love *Smashing Glass & Kicking Ass: Lessons in Success from the Meanest Woman Alive* by Linda Smith, an incredible woman, undefeated litigator, and someone who has real-life lessons we can all benefit from reading.

YOUR SUBTITLE IS THE PROMISE.

What does your book *promise*? What will your reader take away from reading your book? How will they benefit from taking your advice? Will they save money? Make money? Set themselves up for success? Finally write and self-publish their book like a star, raise their profile, and increase their bottom line? You'll craft a subtitle that tells them about your promise in a way that makes them want to immediately pick up and read your book.

Here are a few great examples of well-written subtitles:

- The Power of Habit: Why We Do What We Do in Life and Business
- Grit: The Power of Passion and Perseverance
- Choose Yourself: Be Happy, Make Millions, Live the Dream
- Master Evernote: The Unofficial Guide to Organizing Your Life with Evernote
- Will It Fly?: How to Test Your Next Business Idea So You Don't Waste Your Time and Money

As you can see, each title tells you what the book is about, and the subtitle shares the book's promise and tells you exactly what you're going to get if you read it. A terrific title and solid subtitle, combined with a beautifully designed cover will almost compel an ideal reader to buy (and, of course) read your book.

When titled and subtitled correctly, your reader will move heaven and earth to read it right away … especially if your book has the opportunity to solve a problem or help the reader design or create their ideal outcome!

Bonus: If the book is a gift from you, the author, there is a great chance they will read the book right away. Don't be surprised when you get an email or even a handwritten note from someone who read and appreciated your book.

YOUR KEYWORDS.

While I could write an entire (albeit short) book on the subject of metadata (which includes your book description, book categories, and more), I wanted to be sure to point out the keywords you choose are critical to your book's success. Choosing the right keywords are important for an author to get their books found by Amazon shoppers. Keywords are the words they type into Amazon's search bar when they are looking for their next book, or a book on a specific topic. So, imagine how incredible it would be if your book was at the top of the list when people type in a particular phrase. My friend Dave Chesson created a tool to expedite the process of identifying the best keywords for your book called Publisher Rocket. Publisher Rocket will help you find the exact phrases shoppers type into Amazon when searching for a book on your topic (and even tell you how many people use that phrase when buying their next book). With this tool, you can pick the best keywords for your book and increase the likelihood people find and buy it. Find out more here: https://tinyurl.com/PublisherRocket

Pricing Your Book

How you price your book will be based upon several factors: (a) how other books in your area of expertise are priced, (b) how long it has been on the market, (c) the size of your platform, and (d) how excited your market is to get their hands on the information.

Remember: you are putting your years of education, experience, and knowledge into an easy-to-digest and purchase format others can access for about the cost of a cup of coffee or two. A win-win for both reader and author *in my book*.

Traditionally published ebooks can be as high as $17.99, or even more, and are rarely below $9.99. I believe this is simply because there are so many people that have to get paid out of those dollars. Self-published authors have a distinct advantage because, at the standard 70 percent royalty rate from Amazon, you're making $2.10 even at the low $2.99 price point. The Miracle Morning series is so popular, the books easily sell at $9.99, and *The Martian*, the super-successful science fiction novel by Andy Weir, sells and sells (and sells!) for $8.99 (ebook) and $9.99 (paperback). I've priced most of the books in the Successful Single Mom series at $4.99 (or less), and the six-book boxed set at $9.99 because I'm taking into consideration the fact that single moms are often on a limited budget.

Consider the affluence and discretionary income level of your avatar when pricing your book. Launch strategy comes into play in pricing and requires additional thought and planning.

Paperbacks range from $5.99 on the low-end to $19.99 (or maybe a little more) on the high-end. Page length can be a factor when determining your price, but it is not as important as you might think. My first book, *Tall Order!* (2004 edition), was priced at $14.99. The book was only 77 pages total and was designed to fit in a man's inside suit coat pocket (4" x 7"). The 10th anniversary edition of *Tall Order!* is also priced at $14.99, even though it has been revised, expanded, and updated. The size now is the same as my other books (8.5" x 5.5").

When we launch each book in the Miracle Morning series, the coauthor, Hal, and I put our heads together to determine the best way to get the book in the hands of the people who need and will benefit from it the most. We launched *The Miracle Morning for Writers* at $0.99 for the ebook and sold several thousand copies in the first few days, allowing readers to grab a copy at a nominal price, capitalize on the promise of the book (*How to Build a Writing Ritual that Increases Your Impact and Your Income … Before 8 AM*) immediately.

In our private launch group on Facebook, our early readers shared how they finished writing nonfiction books and novels alike that had been collecting dust for years. It was those initial readers that even today provide the social proof needed to sell lots of books long-term.

When pricing your ebooks and paperbacks, consider the following elements: Your writing style (do you add in lots of meaty content, examples, interviews, reference material, or are you more of a cut-to-chase person) combined with the number of pages and how valuable the content is to the reader factors in heavily. Where you're selling the books matters too. Lots of books or "guides" are sold privately on the authors' websites for between $27 and $99 or more or on other online platforms. One key to your decision is whether competitors' books will be featured alongside yours. If so, you'll need to be in alignment with those books, unless you have a "big name" (large platform and following) or some other special circumstance (such as your book is being turned into a movie or you are appearing on every talk show known to God and man).

Here's a fun fact: Once your paperback starts to sell on Amazon, they will discount it to encourage purchases but still pay you the 45 percent royalty based upon the retail price you set.

You can't go wrong by pricing your book in the middle of the road ($4.99–$7.99 for ebooks and $12.99–$17.99 for paperbacks). The price points are low enough that your readers won't think twice about springing for them (and benefit from them), and you'll sell lots of copies. A true win-win.

If you're thinking of making your book more competitive by lowering the price, consider the fact that the Amazon royalty drops to 35 percent when the price drops below $2.99. And buyers start to wonder if the book has substance if it's priced below that point unless it's a temporary promotional price. Many people believe "you get what you pay for," and if your book is priced too low, they won't buy it out of the fear it will waste both their time and money.

Self-publishing is brilliant in terms of pricing because you can literally change your prices on a daily basis if you want (you won't want to, but you could). You can put your book on sale during certain periods of the year. For example, I make *The Successful Single Dad* available for $0.99 for the ebook and $5.99 for the paperback around Father's Day. Black Friday and Cyber Monday are terrific times to do book sales because the holidays are when people are looking to give books for gifts. It doesn't even have to be a gift-giving holiday. Author Steve Scott offers a Saint Patrick's Day sale every year, which his readers love.

The best way to launch a book varies slightly depending upon subject matter, time of year, and the goals of the author. I share real-time book launch options in my You Must Write a Book LIVE Coaching Course.

PLATFORMS FOR PUBLISHING

As mentioned above, there are multiple platforms on which to publish your book. The mac-daddy of them all is Amazon. Amazon put the ability to self-publish into the hands of anyone who might want to (a-hem, including *you*). Visit HonoreeCorder.com/AmazonLove for how to launch your book effectively on Amazon.

You could do what's called "going wide," where you publish your book on all platforms. This can be a wise choice because it makes your books available through all major online distribution channels and potentially in almost two hundred countries. Each platform has its own nuances and benefits, and as time passes, they are each offering their own incentives for selling through them (such as advertising, special promotions, and more).

You can also have an exclusive relationship with Amazon and choose to enroll in KDP Select. KDP Select requires distribution only through Amazon (so you cannot, according to their terms of services, sell the book anywhere else, including on your own website), and by enrolling you have the option to participate in

Amazon Marketing Services (I talk about this a bit later) and get paid for page reads by Amazon customers who use Kindle Unlimited.

Protect Yourself and Your Intellectual Property

My books are owned by my publishing company, Honorée Enterprises Publishing, LLC. While I am *not an attorney*, I have quite a bit of experience myself and with past clients who have seen a wide range of bad behavior! You will definitely want to consult a business and/or intellectual property attorney (along with your accounting professional) to discuss whether forming a separate entity is wise. In my humble and professional but not legal opinion, your book(s) can and should be the property of an actual company that is owned by you.

There are multiple reasons, chief among them is protecting yourself from personal liability. If properly formed and the corporate formalities are followed, creditors of your entity will most likely be limited to pursuing the assets of the business for debts owed, rather than your personal assets. Also, depending on your goals of owning and operating the business, you may have other very good reasons to form a legal entity for your business. For example, if there is more than one owner of the business, you almost certainly will want to form an entity to memorialize, among other things, how the business will be operated, how you and your fellow owners will manage the business and be compensated, how profits are distributed, how you will handle a possible sale of the business (or other exit strategy), and what will happen if the owners have a falling out (or if an owner dies or becomes incapacitated). Forming an entity will also make it easier to get outside funding (if you need it), establish business credit, compensate key employees with equity (stock options, profits only interests, etc.), and ultimately sell the business.

A separate entity may also provide tax flexibility and benefits now and into the future. For example, there may be a tax advantage to forming separate entities for your passive income (royalties) and your operating income. You may also, depending on your entity, choose to be taxed as a corporation, a partnership, or as a Subchapter S corporation. Again, you should check with your tax and legal professionals for specific advice regarding your particular situation.

I have a terrific attorney (who contributed the above-two paragraphs) and suggest you source one, too. I might even be persuaded to connect you with mine, if you ask nicely and treat him well.

There are some types of insurance one would be wise to purchase, especially if you are providing legal, medical, or financial advice in your books. *You can provide a disclaimer, but that might not be enough.* Again, consult an attorney and also an insurance agent with a specialty in intellectual property and advice.

Having insurance and a legal entity can provide protection for you, your family, and your other assets in the event someone decides they want to hold you liable for advice you share. Even when you provide great advice and have done nothing wrong, that might not stop certain people from shifting blame for unfortunate events. As a friend has told me, you'd probably beat the rap, but you might not beat the ride. Do yourself the favor of being proactive in this arena.

Note: I have a colleague who published a book on company time using company funds. He was under the impression he would be able to do whatever he wanted with the books, including own the intellectual property, and, perhaps most importantly, retain all income from the book. He was *wrong*. Today, he's no longer with the company. But the book is for sale on Amazon, shows him as the author, and his company as the publisher. They've retained all rights to the book and, sadly, all of the proceeds too.

If you work for a company you don't own, be sure to protect yourself and your intellectual property.

Section II: Actions to Take

The section is, shall we say, the "nitty gritty." For each book project, my assistant and I work from the Book Publishing Checklist. It allows me to make sure every single one of what feels like zillions of tasks gets completed (and on time). And yes, I'm sharing it with you (of course). It's included in this book, and you'll also find a link to download a copy you can use at HonoreeCorder.com/YouMustBonuses. The tasks on the checklist are roughly in order, but keep in mind some tasks will need to occur simultaneously (like writing, sourcing an editor, and commissioning a cover). You'll adapt the timeline to fit your publishing goals, which could range from the holy-time-warp-Batman timeframe of 100 days, to a more comfortable six months, or even the *I already have a full-time job* period of a year.

Before I share with you "what to do," let me first say that, if you are a highly-paid professional (you earn in excess of, let's say, $100 or $150 per hour), *your assistant can and should do the majority of the tasks on my book publishing checklist.* You'll notice I said, "my assistant and I," not "I complete the tasks on this checklist." Your book will be a team effort. Don't let me hear later that you hopped on kdp.amazon.com and spent an hour creating an account and uploading your title when your assistant could have done it. Okay?

Okay! If you don't have an assistant, you can still complete all of the tasks necessary. You'll have a bit of a learning curve, but all retail platforms (while time-consuming) are fairly simple to navigate. Just add in some extra time to your timeline to complete everything.

My main job, which is also your main job, is to write the book. Also important is to work with your assistant to coordinate with other members of your team to accomplish each of the tasks needed to publish the book.

The truth is, you need to know which tasks need to be done and that the tasks get done, not necessarily how to do them. If I have it my way, you definitely aren't going to be doing them yourself. Have your assistant download my publishing checklist at HonoreeCorder.com/YouMustBonuses, and then put it in a DropBox folder. This gives you a line of sight regarding what has and hasn't been done. But under no circumstances are you going to do the work yourself (unless you absolutely have to). Right? Promise me. Okay. Please continue.

— 7 —

YOU MUST LAUNCH YOUR BOOK LIKE A CHAMP

*You might think a good book sells itself,
and that is absolutely, 100 percent not true.*

—HONORÉE CORDER

Even before you hold a finished copy of your book in your hands, even before your book is *finished*, the launch of your book must be a dominant thought in your mind.

You might think that your book is "only" going to replace your business card, and therefore you might not need to give it a proper launch. And you would be *so* wrong (sorry). It is important, no matter your desired goals and outcomes for your book, that you give it the full pomp and circumstance it (and you) deserve.

Your goals and outcomes will inspire your launch, and there are many things you can and must do (no matter what) to launch your book successfully.

Book Launch Strategy

Set a Date and Tell the World.

How? Via Facebook, of course … but not only Facebook. Even if you're not using LinkedIn to the fullest, have never "twittered" (correction: tweeted), and have not even heard of Instagram, I bet you've got a Facebook profile. (If you don't, go now to set one up. I'll wait.) Whether you set your publication date as the ink dries on the first jottings of your idea or wait until you've submitted the book to your editor, once you've determined the perfect birthdate for your book, start telling people.

A strong social media presence on thoughtfully selected platforms, carefully curated by you and your assistant, will allow people who otherwise would never have heard of you and your book discover you.

The minute you have finished your book, add it to your email signature. Be sure to add a "hot link" (a link people can click to buy the book), and if you're an Amazon Associate, be sure to use that link so you'll make a few extra cents per purchase. To see an example, go here: HonoreeCorder.com/YouMustBonuses.

Once your front cover is finalized, create a signature including the .jpeg of your book, like I've described above, and add, "Coming soon! My new book …" with a link to either the pre-order page on Amazon or a designated page on your website.

GIVE YOURSELF A HASHTAG.

You might have seen #youmustwriteabook long before you knew a book of the same title was in the works. You can use the title as the hashtag: I have used #businessdating and #visiontoreality as hashtags. Or, you could use a word from the title, like I did with *The Successful Single Mom* and *If Divorce is a Game, These are the Rules*, I simply use #singlemoms and #divorce, respectively. These work because one word is (obviously) shorter and because they are terms people search for when seeking information.

ALL OF THE FORMATS.

A book isn't just a book anymore. As I mentioned earlier, your book has four possible formats: ebook, paperback, audiobook, and hardcover. At the very least, you'll want to produce an ebook and paperback version. Depending upon your goals for the book, you might consider having the audiobook produced as well as a hardcover version (which makes an amazing gift).

It is ideal to launch with every version possible of your book available simultaneously, including the ebook, paperback, and audiobook (and perhaps a hardback through LightningSource).

If you are unable (or unwilling) to do that, you can launch them separately, but I am of the strong opinion the ebook and paperback should launch at the same time (launching a print version at the same time gives you the benefit of having "stabilized pages" for the ebook version, i.e., readers will know exactly how long the book is. Amazon's estimate of ebook pages can vary greatly). Having multiple versions of your book helps you to appear more professional and makes your book look more like a traditionally published one. However, the benefit of not launching in concert is each new version provides another opportunity for you to talk about your book.

The last several book projects I've worked on (mine and the Miracle Morning series) have launched ebook, paperback, and audiobook at the same time. Some readers want all of them, and they want to purchase them simultaneously. Amazon offers Whispersync on some books, which allows people to switch between the ebook and audio versions and keep their place. They also offer a special (read: lower) price for some books if the reader wants to purchase both versions at the same time.

Every reader likes to consume their books according to their personal preferences: some like to listen to the audiobook while driving, doing chores or mindless paperwork, or working out; others highlight the paperback for better learning, retention, and reference; and still others like the ebook version because they can read it anywhere on a device they already have with them.

People will sometimes wait until they can pick up the audiobook to purchase any version. You have to decide which version(s) will work best for you according to your goals for the book.

Suggested Tactics for Your Book Launch

Like deciding which formats work best for your business and your book, you can choose from the individual tactics that follow. However, I highly suggest you use as many as you can manage and all of them if you can swing it. A salad with only lettuce, carrots, a slice of tomato, and a dash of salad dressing is technically still a salad, but it's not a very good salad. The right ingredients in the right amount topped with your favorite dressing make a delicious salad—one you look forward to and one that works for you. These tactics, combined, will provide you with a successful launch and ensure you reach your other business and book goals.

CREATE A PRE-ORDER PAGE AND SET YOUR PRICE FIFTEEN TO NINETY DAYS PRIOR TO LAUNCH.

Your manuscript is finished, cover and layout designed, and your book is *ready*. To begin to create buzz for your book, put it up for pre-order. This will require you to upload the final book for sale on Amazon through KDP. You can do this up to 90 days prior to launch. You can then move to communicating with your list about other important matters.

CONTACT BOOKBUB AND BUCKBOOKS.NET FOR A PROMOTION.

BookBub is the kingmaker of the indie book business. They provide daily deals to their list of subscribers for books that are free or on sale for $0.99, $1.99 or $2.99. Their list is *huge*, and if you are selected for a BookBub promotion, it can help catapult your book into Amazon's stratosphere. Don't lose heart if you aren't selected on the first go-round, most aren't. You can resubmit every thirty days (so be sure to set a reminder in your calendar). Also, BookBub is a bit of a black box—they don't share exactly how they do what they do (proprietary info, no doubt), but if you can get it, it can and will send your book into the top seller region of your category and give it a boost that lasts a while.

BuckBooks.net is a daily service that alerts subscribers to $0.99 books and even has free flash book sales and events. They have a fairly big list, and Shelley Hitz of Training Authors (one of my favorite resources for nonfiction book marketing) used Buck Books with good results. You can read her blog here: http://tinyurl.com/99CentBook.

BUILD YOUR LIST WITH A LEAD MAGNET.

Create interest in you and your book by giving away something of value to prospects and prospective readers in exchange for their email address. In the book business, this is generally called a "lead magnet." Your lead magnet is given in exchange for someone's email address, and doing this over and over serves to build your list. The members of your list are called *subscribers.*

Cultivating your list of subscribers, rather than relying solely on social media to communicate with people who might be interested in your book or services, gives you control over when and how you communicate with them for as long as they stay with you.

You provide access to your lead magnet via a landing page dedicated to this purpose with no other options or content to distract them.

To craft your lead magnet, you can use information contained in the book, or other complimentary information. For example, Steve Scott offers something you might find helpful: *The Bestseller Checklist: 46 Actions to Turn Your Idea into a Bestselling Book.* You'll find it here: Authority.Pub. Steve isn't gathering emails with his lead magnet for one book. In fact, he is an authority in the self-publishing space (and you may remember, my coauthor, with Hal Elrod, of *The Miracle Morning for Writers*).

You can, and should, do the same—not only for the success of your book, but also for the overall health of your business. If, up to this point, you've used old-school networking to develop contacts and business relationships, you've been missing out not only on the benefits of having a book but also the power of the internet to attract new prospects to you.

In case you're stuck on what to offer, the possibilities for what you can use as a lead magnet are limited only by your imagination. It could be a one-page download, short ebook, a checklist, cheat sheet, discount, coupon, or free access to a webinar or online course.

Perhaps you are a divorce attorney, and you're writing a book on collaborative divorce. Your book could be titled *The Joy of Collaborative Divorce,* and your lead magnet could be *The 5 Reasons*

Why Collaborative Divorce Is Your Best Option. You could write the *5 Reasons* as a one-page checklist, a short article, or mini ebook.

A CPA could offer *10 Ways to Make Working with Your Tax Preparer Faster, Easier, and Less Expensive* as a lead magnet for their book *How to Be Your CPA's Favorite Client.*

The idea is to encourage prospective readers, otherwise known as prospective clients, to sign up for your list by sharing their email in exchange for something they want. Jeffrey Gitomer offers access to his weekly sales newsletter, as well as a free ebook, for signing up for his list.

Ask yourself, *what would be incredibly valuable for my potential readers and clients, and what is the best format for them?* Remember to consider your avatar when making this decision.

OFFER TWO FREE CHAPTERS AND WEBSITE PAGE.

You probably have a solid idea for your lead magnet. I want to share another option for post-publication. Use the beginning of your book to pique the interest of prospective readers and clients while simultaneously building your list. You'll use the first two chapters of your book (and everything that precedes them, known as your "front matter," such as the title page, table of contents, introduction, etc.) and create what is known as a "two-chapter opt-in."

Here's an example of the *Prosperity for Writers* two-chapter opt-in: HonoreeCorder.com/Writers. Providing a two-chapter sample will give people a taste of you, your book, and your services, as well as your business approach, style, and sense of humor.

Remember, they will have to join your list to gain access, which means you now have permission to market to them regularly. They may choose to purchase and read your book, which can help them determine if they want to engage you or purchase your services and/or products. Or, they might call to hire you straight away because they feel comfortable based upon the fact that you're an expert with a book. I've had that happen a few times, and it's very cool to realize you're talking to someone who is ready to get started *right now* (especially because I know you're ready right now, too)!

I don't want to get too technical here, but I want to give you what you need to carry this out. It's important! So when you're ready to build your lead magnet and the corresponding pages on your website and set up your email service, have your assistant visit this site: http://tinyurl.com/Hubspot-LandingPage.

EMAIL YOUR LIST.

The more people on your list, the more reach you have in general to help get the word out about your book. Over time, you'll develop "true fans." Very briefly, a true fan is someone who knows, likes (or loves!), and trusts you. They are willing to buy whatever you offer simply because it's yours. They also tend to consider seriously your recommendations for other products and services. If you have 1,000 of these true fans and you offer at least $100 in products and services to them that they buy, then that's income of $100,000 per year (or 100 true fans buying $1,000 worth of products or services), which is a *great* start for an author business. I suggest you read *1,000 True Fans* by Kevin Kelly to understand why this is important.

Use any list you have and use my advice, above, to start building it the minute you read this sentence. Yes, even while you are still contemplating writing your book. (A large list will ensure a healthy and successful business.)

If you don't have a list and need to build one, here are your action steps:

If you haven't already begun to build a list, create an account with Aweber (http://www.Aweber.com), MailChimp, or the service of your choice. A great email service will allow you to email your contacts without hitting their spam filter.

1. Go through your Rolodex, email contacts, that pile of business cards in your desk drawer, and phone, and send an email requesting that people opt in to your list. I use a double opt-in, which requires subscribers to confirm they want to be on my list.

2. If you aren't already, start regularly communicating with your list. When I was a full-time business coach, I emailed my list every Tuesday. I always included easily consumable yet meaty content and kept it low on the "would you like to buy …" These days, I email my different lists once or twice a month. As an expert, you should send content to your subscribers on a consistent basis. A regular email that gives value to your fans will serve to elevate your platform, provide great information, and even build a deeper relationship with each of them. It's the best way to be in touch without actually having to personally be in touch.

Once your list is up and running, you'll want to communicate several times specifically about your book. Before you panic about emailing "too often," remember this: the people on your list have affirmatively chosen to hear from you. They *want* to receive your information, tips, tools, and strategies, as well as updates and breaking news. Well, my friend, your book is all of those things and more! Plus, it is an opportunity for them to support you in your endeavors. I love it when a friend of mine writes a book (this means *you*, by the way) and sends me an email about it.

I suggest you email your list about your book:

- When you form your Advanced Review Team. (More on that shortly.)
- Day of launch

- A week or two after the launch

Just like any other product or service, most people need multiple exposures before they take action. In your first email, let people know your book is going to be available in a week and provide the link where they can purchase it or grab your first two chapters. If your book is appropriate to be given as a gift, much like the book *Giftology* by John Ruhlin, encourage them to purchase a book for a friend, a dozen books for their office, or 25 or more books for their favorite clients.

Then, on release day, share an excited, "My book, [insert title], is available *now*," (and, yup, you'll include a link). Ask them to buy it and share with their colleagues, clients, and on social media.

Finally, wait a week or two and send an update. It could be in conjunction with your regular email, or you could send a special message—you make that call when the time comes. You might share "my book is a hot new release" or "it's #1 or in the top ten in [insert category] on Amazon," or any other good news you can share. They may not have had a chance to grab a copy, so once it's been available for a little while, your message will be a reminder and encourage them to do so (and help keep your book's rank chugging along on Amazon and other online retailers).

LEVERAGE FRIENDS, CONTACT, AND NETWORK.

In addition to your main list, you'll make a separate list of your best contacts, people with large platforms, who would be thrilled to promote your book. How do you know they'd be thrilled? Well, if you have their cell phone number in your phone, and vice versa, and they would take your call if they were available, *you are friends or friendly enough to ask a favor.*

CREATE SHAREABLE SOCIAL MEDIA IMAGES AND POSTS.

If you haven't had a strong social media presence up until this point, now is a great time to set up your twitter, Facebook, and LinkedIn accounts.

There are two equally important facets of social media: the *social* and the *media*. Let's start with the media: that is what you share and is primarily about promotion. You'll use a good number of your posts to tell people where they can buy your book or opt in for two free chapters.

Your graphic/cover designer can use your cover as the inspiration for creating social media graphics in different shapes. The front cover image can be expanded to create an oblong header for a Facebook group. The same square image you use for your audiobook cover can be used as your personal Facebook page image (a.k.a. your profile picture), on Instagram as a post, or even your profile photo.

Your book text can be repurposed into tweets, and you can use ClickToTweet.com to help your advance reader team, fans, and followers help spread the word. Use pre-populated messages that can be used by the launch team or offered as an alternative for folks who can't send email lists. Be sure to include a link to your website's landing page or Amazon so they can buy the book … and by all means, include your hashtag if there are enough spaces left!

Here's an example:

This is your year to become a full-time, prosperous writer! #ProsperityforWriters http://Amzn.to/28Zdo0Z.

Here's the Click-to-Tweet link for the text, above: http://ctt.ec/5Aqob.

I personally love Click-to-Tweet because it is easy to log in using my twitter account, and I can create what I need in less than ten seconds. Ease of use, along with speed of use are important to me, and I know it is to you, too.

Then there's the social part, and believe me, it is equally as important as the media facet. If you post "buy my book," and "hire me!" all the time, people will un-follow, disconnect, and avoid you (and your book). I'm careful to balance my posts and do my best to post as many pictures of my cats, family, and food (usually in that order) as I do links to my books.

While I'm not selling many services these days, when my time was split among coaching, speaking, and crafting books, I had lots to share. I imagine you will, too. While it would be great if I could give you an exact equation, my best advice is for you to begin posting and let common sense be your guide. The social side allows you to engage with family, friends, and yes, business connections. People do business with people they know, like, and trust, and social media can go a long way to help you connect with people in a new, different, and effective way.

One final note about social media: nothing you post *ever* is a secret. Your private or secret Facebook group isn't. It can (and will) be found. To that end, just assume everything and anything you post may at some point be featured on the front of the *New York Times*. Share accordingly. My strategy is to post only positive, upbeat, and encouraging posts. I keep my opinions and my bad days to myself, and know it will serve you to do the same.

AMAZON MARKETING SERVICES ADVERTISING CAMPAIGNS.

Amazon.com has been a leader in allowing anyone to get their message out through self-publishing. They have made the habit of being a book junkie much more affordable. But that isn't all.

Authors who choose to enroll their book in KDP Select, which, as discussed a bit earlier, means you sell your books *exclusively* through Amazon, gain access to Amazon's book advertising platform (among other benefits). It allows them to place a bid on key words, products, or categories.

Much like Google's Ad Words, Amazon's system has become a powerful tool for finding readers outside the author's ordinary sphere of influence.

It takes some time, patience, and testing to develop ads that hit the sweet spot with readers, but it is well worth the effort. You remember my author buddy (and co-author of three books in the *The Prosperous Writer's* Book Series), Brian Meeks, from earlier in this book. He has written a terrific book, *Mastering Amazon Ads: An Author's Guide*. As a former data analyst and six-figure author, he understands how ads, data, and book sales go together. If you're an author who wants to understand Amazon ads for your book, this must go in your to-read pile.

FACEBOOK ADS.

Facebook ads are an incredible resource for self-published authors. Executed correctly, they provide a terrific opportunity to place the most targeted of ads and find readers. Execute *in*correctly, and you can blow through even the biggest of marketing budgets in record time. Since Facebook ads can be targeted to precise specifications, you can get incredibly precise, even if your target is "third-grade teachers who like jellybeans." "Reducing to the ridiculous" is a phrase that comes to mind with Facebook ads; they allow you to target the people who meet your avatar's demographics.

There is one resource I recommend for Facebook ads: Mark Dawson's Facebook Ads for Authors Course.

FORM A PRIVATE, TOPIC-SPECIFIC FACEBOOK GROUP.

Let's suppose your area of expertise, and your book, revolve around sales and selling for women. You could create a Facebook group, perhaps titled Success in Selling for Women, which might also be the same or similar to your book title. Go through your personal and professional contacts, don't forget LinkedIn, and invite prospective group members to join.

Once you have started a group, be sure to post there at least once a day. Do your best to spend some time in the group, commenting on others' posts and providing encouragement. In addition to encouragement, provide what John Lee Dumas calls *value bombs*. Value bombs are key pieces of helpful information. I love value bombs because they inspire me either to try something new or do the thing I already knew about but wasn't doing. Especially if the value bomb tells them the *why* in addition to the *what*, you'll have participants who get involved with your group because people go where they get value and feel welcome. The most successful groups on Facebook are the ones with tons of engagement. Ultimately, you want a group that becomes a community of people with you as the catalyst, the leader, educator, and advisor.

A word of caution: Never add someone to a group without their permission. You can invite them, either through Facebook, or by email, or even by going the old-fashioned way: *use the telephone.* I belong to lots of groups on Facebook, and the majority of them I have chosen to join. Sometimes I am randomly added to a new group without prior knowledge or my permission. And here's what I do when that happens: I immediately leave the group and select the option "block anyone from re-adding you to this group." Even if I might have been interested, the lack of couth exhibited by the person adding me to the group tells me I don't want to be a part of it.

GOODREADS.

Goodreads is *the* hangout for readers. Be sure to create a Goodreads Author Profile and claim your book. Even while your book is in the pre-publishing phase, you can create a profile, participate in on-going discussions, and even start a group (much like on Facebook).

No matter where you find negative reviews, Goodreads or elsewhere, I caution you to not respond. I've heard you're not even a real author until you get a hater (a.k.a. a troll), so welcome one-star reviews and hateful comments with the thought, *I've finally made it! Woohoo!*

USE AN ADVANCED READER TEAM TO SPREAD THE WORD.

Advanced Reader Teams (ARTs) are *awesome*, and when curated correctly, they can make your book launch unbelievably successful. For the launch of *The Miracle Morning for Network Marketers*, I worked with coauthor Pat Petrini to curate an ART of over 550 members. Through a survey, the members opted in to our list, which we used to send almost-daily messages (including videos, quotes, and inspiration) to remind them to read their advance copies, share their favorite passages, purchase the book during the soft-launch day (more on this later), and write their review. We launched with 150 five-star reviews (our goal was at least 100), which helped to propel our book to best-seller status even before our official launch day *and* has kept our book in the top five in its category since then.

Here is your eight-step process for executing a launch team like a pro:

Advanced Reader Team Launch Strategy

Recruit.

Ask people to join a private Facebook group who are interested in being on your advance review team (ART). Send a note to your main email list and ask them to join your ART. I gave mine a spiffy name: The Review Crew. Create an opt-in page or a survey. Make sure you let them know that in exchange for receiving a *free* advance copy of your book, they are asked to provide a review on Amazon and Goodreads. During your soft launch (the day your book goes live, which is three to four days before the publicized date of your book launch), you should price the book at $0.99 specifically so that your ART can purchase it (more on that later). Be sure to review Amazon's policies where reviews are concerned, so you don't run afoul and end up having them deleted or worse (end up in Amazon jail).

Your ART gets their advance review copy two to three weeks prior to the launch. The more time you give them, the better chance they will have actually read the book prior to your launch day and have their review ready to go. One option is to have them fill out a survey in order to join your ART. For example, check out Pat Petrini's version for *The Miracle Morning for Network Marketers:* http://tinyurl.com/PatsOptin. You can also simply invite them to join your ART, which is what I usually do. Here's a link to my opt-in page: http://honoreecorder.com/reviewcrew/.

How much you put into your ART will depend on how much time you have to devote to it, what else you have to offer, and how selective you want or need to be with your participants.

SEND UPDATES.

When they join, send them a couple updates letting them know the book is almost ready and they'll have it on "Saturday the 14th" so they can start reading. If you give them an anticipated date, you'll find they are ready to begin reading because they expect it and make room on their calendars for it.

SEND THE BOOK.

At least three weeks before the launch, send your ART an advance review copy. Sometimes, my books are ready months in advance. If that's true in your case, feel free to send the review copies a couple of months ahead of time. The benefit of the extra time is multi-faceted: you will give your ART additional time to read, have time to correct errors or typos, and allow extra time to put any additional marketing ideas into practice.

You'll want PDF, .mobi (for Amazon Kindle), and .epub (for the iPad and all other digital readers). I use BookFunnel (http://bookfunnel.com) to deliver my advance copies for a couple of reasons: it isn't expensive and has quite a number of options for use. Some people are truly tech savvy and know how to side load a book onto their favorite electronic device. Others find this challenging. Make your life and that of your ART easy by providing them a simple solution. Remember, the confused mind says no.

ASK YOUR ART TO READ IT AS SOON AS POSSIBLE.

From one author to another, you've got to stay on top of your ART. If you send them the book and expect them to, of their own accord and with no reminder, read the book and leave a review, you will most likely be sadly disappointed. Even the most responsible and organized people get distracted by everything from a new project to a kitten video.

As I mentioned above, Pat Petrini was the best I've seen at regularly communicating with his ART. He sent a video message every couple of days, provided content, bonuses, and extras that didn't make it into the book. He stayed in touch over the three weeks prior to the launch.

Plan to send a reminder to your entire ART every day or two prior to the launch. Go to http://tinyurl.com/PatsNMVideo for one of the videos Pat sent to our ART for *The Miracle Morning for Network Marketers*. As you can see, he shot the video wherever he happened to be at the time. In other words, there's no need to be in a studio, wear a fancy outfit, or have your hair and makeup done. Your ART is a group of your friends, family, and fans so be your authentic self in your videos and emails.

1. **Capture the best of the book.** Start a thread in your ART Facebook group and ask the members to leave their favorite quotes and ideas there. You can do this by asking a question, or posting one of your favorite parts of the book, and asking them to do the same. What you're going for with regular posts is group engagement. The more people post in the group, the more often each member of the ART will get notifications that serve as a reminder to read, buy, and review the book. Trust me, this works wonders.

2. **Social media magic.** Turn the best quotes into shareable social media graphics. I use the app WordSwag to turn photos and quotes into shareable posts. While someone might entirely miss words, a picture will grab their attention. Combined with a memorable quote, your photo can be liked and shared over and over.

3. **Continue to cultivate your ART.** Here's a complete list of action steps:

a) Post daily videos.

b) Send those videos by email to the list.

c) Give resources to share.

d) Start threads at least once a day.

e) Give encouragement, celebrate special moments, and be positive whenever you can.

f) Make it easy for them to share your message by providing tweets and photo posts.

g) Ask them to change their FB photo to a square graphic of your book for the day (it will show up on their timeline, and all their contacts will see it). You'll need a 2400 x 2400 pixel square version of your book cover for this, which your graphic designer can easily provide (you'll need it if you do an audio version of your book as well).

Exponential exposure is what you're after here. You never know when someone will see your graphic and take action by reading your book or hiring you.

4. **Launch.** As you build up to the launch day, provide ongoing cheerleading, but also give as much value as you possibly can. Yes, your ART has received a free copy of your book, and that's great; however, they've given you hours of their time by reading it. That's a *w* in the win column for you, without question. So ask yourself what else you can provide, and do more than they can possibly expect. You'll find that they will do more than you expect.

Turn the launch into an event, a book launch party on Facebook. This event is completely separate from the pre-launch group. Invite your ART as well as *all* your other contacts to the event. Ask them to stop by on the day of your launch to say a few words, post pictures of themselves with your book, or share their favorite paragraph or quote. Give away prizes throughout the day. You could give away something you usually charge a lot for. In my case, I've given away a coaching session, a copy of a different book, Starbucks gift cards, and even some "Cult of Honorée" merch.

Launch Pricing Strategy

You might wonder how you should price your book during the launch and if the price should be different than where it settles later. Different types of books will need different pricing strategies during the launch, yet there are a few givens, pricing strategies that stand the test of time and ones you can use in your launch.

- Three days before your hard launch is the date of your soft launch. These three days are critical for a few reasons: (1) Pricing your book at $0.99 between the soft and hard launch dates will enable more members of your ART to purchase the book at the lowest price possible and write verified reviews. I promote the soft launch and $0.99 price point only to the ART (and tell them so). They appreciate it and go out of their way to buy and review.
- **Note**: I have it on good authority that verified reviews carry five times the impact of an unverified review. The sale counts as a sale for ranking purposes, the price point is easily digestible for anyone, and the review provides third-party validation. It's a win-win-win. Even if Amazon's algorithms didn't reward you for verified purchases, potential readers can see the label, and they know what it means.

The exception to this pricing strategy for the soft launch would be if you were accepted for a BuckBooks.net or BookBub.com promotion. The promotion will drive your price before, during, and after the promotion. If that happens, send me an email, and we'll discuss!

- Raise your price to $2.99 on your official launch day, and leave it there for about three days. At $2.99, you get the 70 percent royalty rate from Amazon, so you're making around $2.10 per book (versus $0.35 at the $0.99 price point). For days four through six, keep an eye on your Amazon rank and sales. If sales are strong, you can either ride the wave of a lower-priced book for an even higher ranking, or you can slowly raise the price by a dollar every day or so.

- You'll want to raise your book's price to between $3.99 and $5.99 on days seven through ten, depending on where you plan to permanently set the price. Use your Amazon ranking to determine if the price should be raised or not. If you are still selling a fair amount of books (20–25 a day), even as you raise the price, you can continue to raise it at regular intervals until you've hit your pre-determined full price.

A solid launch sets the stage for a successful and long life for your book. But the initial launch period will quickly come to an end, and then the long-term (read: *forever*) and continuous marketing of your book begins.

Think of your book like a good friend or happy marriage: the more love and effort you put into it, the more you get out of it.

The next phase of your book's life is basically the rest of the book's life … a successful launch sets the stage for a long and successful product in your arsenal that will provide new business and income for you and value and assistance for its readers.

— 8 —

YOU MUST PLAN TO MARKET YOUR BOOK

I didn't come this far only to come this far.
—TOM BRADY, NFL QUARTERBACK AND
FIVE-TIME SUPER BOWL CHAMPION

At some point in the near future, you will hold your finished book in your hands. You will have successfully written, published, and launched your book, sold some copies, and perhaps even already garnered some new business. You'll be tempted to take a deep breath followed by a deep sigh of relief. You might even think, *Thank goodness that's done!*

I don't want to boil your bunny or anything like that, but I have to point out that you have now moved on to the next phase of your book's life: marketing.

Think about it like childrearing: pregnancy is the easy part (and lasts a relatively short time) and raising your child is the real work. Well kids, writing your book is like being pregnant. Sometimes you're bloated and nauseated; other times you feel amazing and like you've got the world by the (*ahem*) tail. But without question, a book no one knows about might as well not exist.

And you haven't come this far only to come this far. So let's sell some books, raise awareness about your awesomeness, and make you some money, shall we?

The Marketing Begins

Whether your book had a launch that could only be described as epic (i.e., you are now a *New York Times* Best-Selling Authorand household name) or you had a small launch consisting of an even smaller mailing of about 50 books, the future of your book, along with the benefits it can provide you, your business, and its readers, lies solely in what you do from this day forward.

I made incorrect assumptions after I published the original *Tall Order!* I had heard "if a book isn't successful within three months, it's a loser." Not just successful as in "I've sold lots of copies" or "it made a list" (like the *New York Times* or *Wall Street Journal*), or was being sold in bookstores. The three-month rule only applies to traditional publishing. With self-publishing, your book's life is solely dependent upon you and your marketing and sales efforts.

So once the excitement and newness had worn off, I didn't talk about or share my book very much at all. I had ordered 15,000 copies. The remaining 3,500 copies collected dust for a few years after the initial launch. While I would give them out a few at a time, I didn't execute many of the tactics I use dozens of books and many years later.

Think of your book like you would a business card: you wouldn't order 2,000 cards and then not give them away. You have them available to give away just about any time someone requests one.

Think of your book as your new business card but also your brochure and website rolled into one.

First Things First

I am, very soon, going to blow your noodles when I share my ninja strategies. But never one to put the cart before the horse, it would be a disservice to you if I simply shared my tactics and didn't help you set the stage to execute them successfully.

It is a great idea to define the goals for your book and then identify the strategies that will work best for you to accomplish those goals. I'm going to share what has worked well for me, and they will either work great for you or help nudge your creative juices and define some that will yield you the new readers and clients or customers you desire.

Finding new clients can be hard work, requiring determination, endurance, strength, and flexibility. We're on the clock here, and time is of the essence. You've taken time away from your business to write your book, so you can generate more business in an effective and efficient way.

As you know, prospects must be exposed to you, and now your book, a number of times before what they see registers and they feel compelled to take action. And they'll need to hear about you a few times more before they actually take action.

When you play your cards right and put the book into the right hands, you could soon experience the power of going viral. There's nothing like *You have GOT to read this book!* to encourage someone to read it and feel compelled to hire you.

But you have to get the book into the hands of that first person who thinks your book rocks and should jump to the top of the pile. The number one way a book is discovered is through a personal recommendation. The challenge is getting your books to enough people to allow this buzz to occur.

Your Book Marketing Plan

I was a business and executive coach for more than a decade, and coaches are known for helping clients set great goals and create the solid plans that support their attainment. When I started, my plan consisted of *identify seven things to do every day to market my book,* and I did them. Not much of a plan, really, in retrospect. More like random action taken with my fingers crossed. While those seven actions I took every day worked like a charm, they weren't based on a vision, outcome, or a specific goal. I can't let you write the book you're excited to write without encouraging you to put incredible forethought into what you want out of it.

Taking action without a plan is a huge mistake, and I missed a very important aspect of a great plan: the vision, or *what did I ultimately want from the book.* There are three questions to ask yourself as you think about crafting a vision:

1. Do you want to sell lots of books?
2. Do you want more business?
3. Do you want to sell lots of books *and* gain more business?

I'm going to assume you want both, but just in case you want one or the other, I've crafted two complete chapters, one for each desired outcome. Once you've completed your plan, you can read either or both of the next two chapters depending upon your desired outcome.

Based upon the vision for your books, another integral aspect of your plan is going to be your goal. What did I ultimately want from marketing my first book? Money? Sure! But how much? I didn't say and didn't know. Sales? Well, duh, but I didn't identify *how many* I wanted. Theoretically, I would've been happy with any result, which is absolutely not true.

I took non-directed action without a specific outcome in mind. Lucky for me, even though I didn't know what I didn't know, my tactics worked. Even without a strategy, I was successful based upon my non-identified outcomes. I made enough money to feel like my time, money, and energy had been well spent. But I often wonder, *what if I had based my tactics on a solid strategy? What if I'd have had a concrete plan with action steps based on the goals set forth in the plan?*

You're reading this book, and writing your own, in part because you want to find more clients or customers as quickly and easily as possible. To do that, you're going to need a plan, a goal or three, and action items that support the goals and the plan. Make sense? Then let's get on with it, shall we?

Creating an Action Plan

I'm going to walk you through my process for determining my goals and the corresponding action items to achieve them. I've got a blank, downloadable plan for you HonoreeCorder.com/YouMustBonuses.

What Do You Want?

The first step in any action plan is to determine what exactly you want. Once you have a book idea in mind, knowing your desired outcome for writing it is key. Once you've published and launched your book, you've achieved those two outcomes, and it's time to replace them with a clear picture of what you desire long term.

Four logical outcomes, or goals, make sense in this context: you want to sell x number of copies, make $x,xxx amount of money from book sales, acquire x new customers/clients, and/or make $xx,xxx in new business. In my book *Prosperity for Writers*, I recommend identifying your monthly nut (that is, the amount of money you need to meet your expenses each month) and then multiplying that number by 1.5, which becomes your personal financial income goal. Identifying your new client revenue or even a personal income goal will help you to determine the action items that will serve to make those goals a reality.

I strongly suggest you set two goals, one based upon the other: your financial income goal and the number of sales required to achieve it.

I'm going to use $10,000 a month or $120,000 per year as an income goal. If you've made $120,000 at any point in your life, this probably sounds like a solid number. But if you saw that number and your head exploded, let me present the number to you in another way: $328.77 per day. I like round numbers, so instead of $328.77, we're going to use $330.00 and give you an immediate raise to $120,450 per year. (You're welcome.)

A daily income of $330.00 per day is the sale of just 95 books at $4.99 or 47 books at $9.99 on Amazon with their 70 percent royalty rate. But while the clock is ticking on the amount of time you have to read and get value from this book (and write your own), there is no shot clock on how quickly you must get to $330 a day, or whatever you've determined your number to be. While of course you want to get there as quickly as possible, it will take as long as it takes, and I'm here to tell you *it's okay for it to take as long as it takes.*

Your Action Plan

Now that you've identified what you want from your book, you can get down to the business of creating your very own action plan, which you can populate with your numbers and intended action items.

I've used big numbers in this plan on purpose because I'm a big thinker, and I believe in abundance. If at any time the numbers seem too big or overwhelming, *simply change them to fit you.* You may not want to do anything more than make enough to be a full-time writer, and that's fantastic. Doing what you love isn't all about the money. It's mostly about being able to make enough money to do what you love. Your first action plan could be to make an additional $1,000 a month from your book and new business, instead of $10,000 (or even $100,000), so you'll just divide all of the numbers by 10. Start where you are, make incremental increases as desired, rinse and repeat. Fair enough?

On the flip side, perhaps you are among those who have already made $10,000 a month and are looking to go to your next level. Good for you! This action plan works just as well for scaling up, regardless of the intended size of your business or income.

Goal-setting: Now you most likely have a number (or several) in mind and it's time to memorialize your intended target. Determine the amount of money you want to make in a year (it could be your monthly nut times 1.5, or you could identify you just want to make enough to take a fantastic vacation every year—completely up to you). Divide that number by 365.

Your total income goal will be the total you expect from on-going business, as well as book sales and new business as a result of your book.

Your annual number is your Goal #1. Your daily number is your Goal #2.

What you've got now are your target numbers.

I've provided an example action plan to get you started:

ACTION PLAN EXAMPLE

What I want from my book: *I am a full-time writer, earning in excess of $10,000 per month from my book and, as a result, $55,000 per month from my business.*

Goal #1: $120,000 Annual income = $10,000 per month

Goal #2: 95 total ebooks and print books sold per day

ACTION ITEMS:

1. Do 1 podcast interview every three days (122 total)
2. Add 5000 people to my email list (13.69 per day)
   a) Update opt-in

Revise auto-responder sequence. You'll find an example at (yup, you guessed it): HonoreeCorder.com/YouMustBonuses

Have twice daily updates in private Facebook group. (Use Bufferapp.com to schedule.)

Post on personal timeline four times per week

1. One blog post per week
2. Read top 100 other books in my genre, write reviews on Amazon and Goodreads.

3. Leave books/bookmarks/postcards in various locations (elevators, bookstores, etc.).
4. Write 2000 words per day in current work in progress to keep with my schedule to publish by [date].

You can download a blank version at HonoreeCorder.com/YouMustBonuses.

I sincerely hope you take the time to create your action plan. Mostly, I want you to execute it! Many an awesome plan has collected dust instead of coming to life, and in your case, that would be tragic! We know that because you bought this book and took the time (your most precious resource) to read it, and you probably have started, if not finished, your own action plan.

Just as I want you to create and execute your plan, I want your words to find the readers who will love them and, as a result, hire you. I highly encourage you to shed any limiting beliefs that stand in your way, tune into (and turn up!) the inner voice that is cheering you on, and go for it 100 percent.

If limiting beliefs are getting in the way of your getting down to business, you might want to check out *Prosperity for Writers*, the book or the course, to help you eliminate any beliefs you have that aren't serving you (you'll find links in the Resources Section at the back of this book for both as well as all of my other books). This is not about selling you another product; it's about getting whatever you need to apply the one you hold in your hands. If this is a problem for you, do whatever you need to do to get back on track.

The only thing standing between you and the readers and clients who will be delighted to find you is, well, not one thing. It's time to market your book!

Return on Time Investment (ROTI)

It is important for me to note that you can try many different marketing activities for your book. Some things you do will yield great results, and others not so much. I call the results you get from the time you spend on your book your return on time investment (ROTI). You want to spend your time so that you get a lot of bang for your buck, but in this case, your buck is actually your minutes. Let me give one quick example of bad versus good ROTI:

- Doing a book signing, or even going on a book tour sounds like a big, sexy thing to do. The problem is, until you have a private jet and own properties in 50 major cities, you're going to endure an unending string of hotel rooms, commercial airline travel (which, these days, is *super fun* ... not!), and eating all of your meals out. Yup, this is a fantastic adventure for a few days or weeks, but at some point, don't you just want to fall into a deep, cozy sleep in your own bed? I know I do! And, all of that effort results in the sale of a few dozen or maybe even a few hundred copies at best. Gross profit: $200-$500. Net profit: less than $0 because you probably have a huge balance on your credit card. Yup, you guessed it—bad ROTI.

- Doing a teleseminar or podcast interview. From the comfort of your own couch (and yes, you can still shower, eat, and sleep in your own bed with no interruptions, boarding passes, or over-priced room service), you can talk to countless people around the world about your book, why it's wonderful, why they should read it, *and* why they should hire or buy from you. With a live event, if someone can't attend, you lose the ability to connect with them. That's not a problem with podcast appearances: Your potential readers and clients can listen with the same device they carry in their pocket or purse at all times: their phone. ROTI = *awesome*.

Sometimes an identified action item that sounds fun and amazing is actually a horrendous waste of time, and you'll wish you had made up some lame excuse like food poisoning or your cat needing an emergency appendectomy so you can be spared the torture of whatever thing you're stuck doing. (Or is that just me?) And, sometimes an identified action item is truly fun and amazing. My point is this: don't just identify action items; you have to do them while paying attention to whether they are worth your time, money, and effort.

And let me rant about *time* for just a minute. It seems to me that most people are confused. They are under the illusion it would be better to spend their time instead of money because "they can't afford to spend money." But here's the truth: they have it backwards, and maybe, so do you! You do *not* have an unlimited amount of time. In fact, I want to thank you for spending your time reading this book, because once time is spent, you can never get it back. Money, on the other hand, can come at any time, and if you're on my prosperity wavelength at all, you believe that when you spend money, even more money is on its way to you. I digress, yet I feel like it's an important point to make. Let me say it another, more positive and less snarky way. *Be doubly as mindful of how you spend your time as how you spend your money.* You can always get more money, but time is finite, and once it has been spent, it is gone forever.

In the next two chapters, I'm going to cover marketing your book and marketing *with* your book. Before you head there, if you haven't already, take a moment to write down your goals. The next two chapters will help you cement your plan for getting your book into the hands of prospective readers and clients.

In chapter 9, I cover both basic and advanced strategies for selling books. If your sole reason for writing a book is to get more customers, your inclination might be to skip the next chapter, but I encourage you to read it anyway. Unless you have an unnatural aversion to money, you might find creating an additional stream of income from your book can be easier and more fun than you think.

In chapter 10, I share how to use your book as a lead magnet, a way to attract and engage new clients or customers. Hands down, having a book is going to be one of the most, if not the most impressive tool in your sales kit.

– 9 –
YOU MUST MARKET YOUR BOOK

*Do something every day to market each
of your books for three years.*
—JOHN KREMER

Writing a book and selling a book are two entirely different challenges. The best book in the world won't do you, your business, or your prospective clients any good collecting dust. I want you to sell as many books as you possibly can, which allows you to help as many people as possible.

Best Book Marketing Strategies:
Awesome Ways to Find Book Buyers, Readers, and Raise Your Profile

These next eight strategies are specifically for selling books, lots and lots of books. I'm focusing on an awesome ROTI here. You could purchase distribution into bookstores, of course. But the following tactics are specifically designed to help you sell books directly (in person or on your website) and indirectly (through Amazon or other online retailers).

USE A FREE TWO-CHAPTER OPT-IN.

Remember the two-chapter opt-in you created to launch your book? Well, it's not just for launching the book. As a matter of fact, this strategy is one of my favorites for long-term book marketing because it can help people find your book for years to come. I know the person who opts in is possibly interested in reading my book, and the first couple of chapters will help them decide for sure. But no matter what, I now have their email address and can stay in touch with them, market to them, and ultimately develop a relationship with them. If your potential readers like what they read, they will probably purchase your book (and any future books you might pen).

To help people find your two-chapter opt-in, you'll want to add it to your ongoing social media postings. Twitter, Facebook, and LinkedIn are three of my favorites for this one.

Add a link to your email signature, when possible. Something like this example is ideal:

Honorée Corder

Author, Speaker, Coach

Have you read my new book, *You Must Write a Book?* Get two free chapters here and buy it <u>here</u>. {add link}

MAKE THE ASK.

Ask your best contacts and strategic partners, "Would you like to buy between 10 and 100 books?" As I mentioned earlier, I asked this very question of just about everyone in my network when I published my first book in 2004, sold 11,000 paperback copies, and it took me just three weeks. I made hundreds of calls and sent dozens of emails to accomplish this task. I was fortunate in that I had lots of contacts who quickly read the book and felt it would add value to their companies or organizations and bought many directly from me.

Before you ask someone to buy your book, especially in quantity, determine the depth of your relationship. Asking too soon can do more harm than good to a relationship in its infant stage. Long-term clients or strong strategic partner relationships (and of course, your mom) will probably be delighted to help you, newer friends and contacts might be willing to purchase a large quantity of books if you give them a copy first and allow them the time to read it.

Here's the strategy, broken down into key steps:

1. Make a list of your best business relationships and call them one by one.
2. Tell them you have a new book and ask if they would like a complimentary copy. Be willing to give them a book to review first. In fact, if the relationship is deep enough,

some of those on your list might be great candidate for your ART.

3. Ask if they want a digital or paperback copy and immediately send them the book. It's a great idea to use an excel spreadsheet to track this.
4. Follow up in three weeks to ask if they've had a chance to read the book. If yes, ask the magic question, "Would you like to buy between 10 and 100 books?" If no, tell them you'll be back in touch soon. Wait another three weeks. Rinse and repeat.

BECOME A PODCAST GUEST.

No matter the subject matter of your book, you will find podcasts that need expert guests, and you my friend, are now an author (which makes you an expert). Do a search for podcasts with a business focus, and you'll see what I mean! With dozens of new podcasts born every day, you won't have a shortage of places you can share your knowledge. And yes, you can even do a search for podcasts in your particular niche and perhaps find dozens who would love to have a new author as a guest.

I love podcasts for several reasons. First, I have knowledge and information that is valuable to the shows' listeners, and my job is show up and have a conversation with the host. Second, podcasts live forever. You can share a podcast an unlimited number of times and for as long as you like.

Hal Elrod appeared on more than 200 podcasts in the three years after *The Miracle Morning* was released, and the success of the book and his speaking career is remarkable. Before his book, he charged $5,000 for a keynote, and now 300+ keynotes later, he charges $25,000 or more.

I've done more than 100 interviews (you can find many of them at HonoreeCorder.com/Media), which I continue to promote. While some people want to appear only on big and established podcasts, my rule is no podcast is too big or too small. You never know when or where your next reader or client is going to come from, and it just might be the brand-new podcast with seven listeners.

A note on new podcasts: If the podcast is successful, fans of the podcast will go back and consume every episode. Don't assume the new podcast with only a few listeners isn't a great place for you to share your expertise. You'll gain interview experience and an interview you can share with others. You win no matter what because you now have an audio you can share to help promote your book.

In addition, some of your fans will want to listen to every interview you do. You can help bring exposure to the podcast you appear on (win-win), and you can find new people who benefit from your knowledge and expertise (also win-win).

It's actually quite easy to get on podcasts. The following are your action steps to appear on as many podcasts as possible:

1. Identify podcasts with the same target audience as your book and expertise. I focus on business and self-publishing podcasts. My soon-to-be author client Linda Smith is having great success appearing on podcasts focusing on business and women's empowerment.
2. Send an email introduction, telling the host who you are and what you have to offer their audience.

When the host expresses interest, provide them with your bio, headshot, and interview sheet. You'll find an example of one here: HonoreeCorder.com/YouMustBonuses.

A few other quick pointers: (1) Be your authentic self on interviews. You have expertise that others want. Share as much as you can as openly as you can. (2) Have a great microphone. I suggest the Logitech ClearChat Comfort/USB Headset H390, which is affordable (less than $30 on Amazon), comfortable, and works very well. (3) Be sure to mention your book (and ask the host to do the same in the introduction and as they close the show). (4) Have a URL you share on every show, such as HonoreeCorder.com/Writers.

OFFER BLOGGERS ADVANCE READER COPIES.

Research bloggers who love to read and write about books in your area of expertise. Providing them with a copy of your book will allow them to read it and share it with their audience.

BECOME A HARD SOURCE.

I'll discuss public relations (PR) as an option for you to sell books in a moment, but one of the best ways to get the word out about your book that I've found is to become a source for the media through Help-a-Reporter-Out (HelpaReporter.com). Media outlets in all forms and all over the world seek sources for the stories they write and produce. Reporters (and other people who need particular information) post what they are talking and writing about and request input from those who can speak intelligently about it. Visit HelpaReporter.com to learn more and become a source.

ADD YOUR BOOK TO YOUR LINKEDIN PROFILE.

Build out your LinkedIn profile to include all of your education and experience. Also add your book to the publications section. It will show up in your timeline when you make the addition and round out your profile in an impressive way.

SPEAKING OF LINKEDIN ...

As a business professional, you should have a fully-tricked out LinkedIn profile. With any luck (and by luck, I mean lots of hard work and terrific timing), your book will spur quite a bit of interest in you. Besides Google, and even by way of this search engine, LinkedIn is quite possibly a prospective client's first stop. In the vetting process, they will want answers to their pressing questions, including the following: Where did the professional/author go to school? What else have they published? Has anyone written a glowing endorsement? How long have they been in their particular position?

A sparse LinkedIn profile can be likened to a publishing expert with two books that have three reviews each and an Amazon rank in the millions. In other words, *no sale*. Literally. Your book can replace your business card and even close the sale. Yet, a solid LinkedIn profile can close the loop in someone's mind, leaving no question about whether you mean business and are indeed the person they must hire.

Here are five critical action steps for maximizing your LinkedIn profile for both book sales *and* marketing with your book (which I cover in-depth in the next chapter):

1. Set up a complete profile. The basic idea here is to not leave any gaps. Fill in each and every section, using the Profile Strength Indicator as a guide (your goal is "all-star").

2. Have a professional photo *and* include your book cover image.

3. Connect with the right people. The old Assyrian proverb applies here: "Tell me who your friends are, and I'll tell

you who you are." Connect with other business authors, other high-profile individuals in your field, and of course, all your past and current clients.

4. Collect endorsements and recommendations. Just like good old-fashioned job recommendations, your prospective clients can see who has gone before them, and how they felt about it!

5. Participate in a special interest group. Groups on LinkedIn are a terrific place to interact with key players in your industry, which will help you to make more connections (see #3) and become an influencer.

Of course, the time to have started your LinkedIn profile was when you began your career (or the first available date). But if you're thinking, *I've done almost nothing with LinkedIn*, something I've heard quite a bit, it is truly all good. Kind of like saving for retirement, the next best day to start is today. While you're still thinking about what book you must write, you can spend time beefing things up over on LinkedIn.

CAPITALIZE ON HOLIDAYS CORRESPONDING WITH YOUR BOOK.

If there are federal, religious, traditional, or informal holidays related to your book, be sure to build a promotional campaign to heighten awareness.

For example, around Mother's Day, I promote *The Successful Single Mom* books. At the end of each year, and the beginning of the next, I promote *Vision to Reality* and *Tall Order!* because I know people are making New Years' resolutions and setting goals. It seems every single day (at least here in the US) is National Something-or-Other Day. Belly Laugh Day is January 24, and look what I found at Checkiday.com: today, July 3, 2016 is American Redneck Day, Disobedience Day, National Build a Scarecrow Day, National

Chocolate Wafer Day, National Compliment Your Mirror Day, National Eat Beans Day, and (last but not least), Stay Out of the Sun Day. That last one is a bit ironic, if you ask me, since it's also Independence Day weekend, and lots of people are hanging out at the beach, or on their boat, or on vacation somewhere *in the sun*. I digress, but I'm sure you can see my point: there are plenty of holidays (real and imagined) you can use as a tie in for your book.

You could even "go ninja" with your book and proclaim a national day of your own. I mean, who's going to stop you? Who is going to say it isn't National Fresh Socks Day or National Buy a House Day or even National Adopt a Guinea Pig Day? Seriously, you could, if you wanted to, decree a day to help shine a spotlight on yourself and your book. In fact, I suggested this to Jon Vroman, founder of The Front Row Foundation. During the writing of this book, he was also hard at work on his first book. What better way to gain the attention his charitable foundation and book deserve than to have National Front Row Day!? Now, every August 8th is National Front Row Day, so be sure to check out Jon's book, *The Front Row Factor: Transform Your Life with the Art of Moment Making*. I know you won't regret living life in the Front Row!

I use Black Friday and Cyber Monday along with major holiday weekends where retailers go wild. And, of course, my birthday (which I consider a national holiday), when I price all of my books at $0.99.

You can find or create many unique and interesting days that will serve to raise awareness about your books and, most importantly, sell them.

Public Relations

As a businessperson, you have (regardless of size) a marketing budget. It serves you well to use a healthy portion of your marketing budget to get the word out about your book since it is the best piece of marketing material you've got, *and* it will do a lot of the heavy lifting when it comes to convincing a prospective client you're *the one* they should hire.

If you're in business for yourself, new to business, or simply have a limited marketing budget, you can still get some fairly decent media exposure by developing a small campaign to get featured on local morning and evening news shows and in local publications. Morning shows are always looking for the "local person makes good" story, and a local professional publishing a book is definitely you making good! Use the same email series and documents you use to book yourself on podcasts to connect with local reporters and other media personalities. Who knows, it just might be practice for regional or even national exposure. Which leads me to …

Hiring an Expert to Help Make You More of an Expert

With enough of a budget, you can hire a public relations expert, preferably one who is familiar with the book business, and in particular, the indie book business. Gabrielle Torello, PR and Communications Consultatnt (gabtpr@gmail.com) was kind enough to answer a few questions about working with a PR firm.

Q1. What is the budget range for an author who wants national PR?

The cost of a national PR campaign can range anywhere from $3,000 per month to upwards of $6,500 per month (and a select few publicists charge by the hour), depending on whether an author is looking to work with a freelancer or an agency. An independent contractor is typically the least expensive way to go, and there are a lot of wonderful, experienced professionals out there. On the other hand, working with an agency will give you the muscle of a larger organization that will have more resources to devote to your project.

Another factor in pricing is the amount of services an author wants. If you're interested in landing speaking opportunities or having book signings arranged, you can expect to pay more per month. Many freelancers will insist on a contract of at least three months, and most agencies would prefer not to take on projects of less than six months' duration. It takes time to plan and execute an effective campaign.

Q2. COULD YOU ALSO COMMENT ABOUT THE DIFFERENT TYPES/LEVELS OF SERVICE YOU PROVIDE (A MENU OF OPTIONS, IF YOU WILL)?

The agency I work with, Grand Communications, is a full-service boutique PR agency based in New York City. We orchestrate effective publicity and social media campaigns for both indie and traditionally published authors, based on the needs of each individual client. A full press campaign will often include strategizing with the author; drafting press releases, bios, pitch letters, fact sheets, and other materials that help us communicate the story to the media and pique their interest in the author and their title(s); brainstorming creative angles for outreach; developing targeted media lists, leaving no stone unturned in pitching and pursuing both local and national print, broadcast and online press opportunities; and providing press updates.

Q3. WHILE YOU CAN'T MAKE ANY PROMISES, CAN YOU SHARE WHAT RESULTS AN INDIE AUTHOR CAN TYPICALLY EXPECT FROM HIRING THE RIGHT PR FIRM?

I wish that I could give you a general rule of thumb on results, but it's the nature of the business that I can't. The beautiful thing about publicity is that it's an organic way for an author to reach readers, but unfortunately, there's no guarantee—unless you're an

A-list celebrity. What any dedicated PR professional worth their salt can promise is that they will leverage all of their close connections (and aim to make more!) on your behalf, look for unique angles and take advantage of what's happening in the world to make your story relevant to reporters and producers, and aggressively follow up on pitches and leads. That being said, if you have an interesting story to share and have written a wonderful book on a topic that people want to hear about, you can expect the media to take notice.

Q4. HOW DO YOU KNOW IF A PR PROFESSIONAL/FIRM IS THE REAL DEAL?

My advice would be to start by asking other indie authors for recommendations on PR professionals they've successfully worked with in the past. When you've identified a few agencies or freelancers, check out their websites or LinkedIn profiles to learn what author clients are on their roster. It's helpful to have a phone call, or better yet, an in-person meeting, if at all possible. It's very important to "click" with the people that you might be working with to help get the word out about your book. Be sure that they're comfortable working with indie authors. Ask to see press clips. Have they gotten a client on late night TV? *Today* or *Good Morning America*? In the *New York Times* or *Wall Street Journal*? It's also a good idea to get a detailed scope of work or proposal outlining the suggested PR plan so you can get an idea of how they work and whether they have the capability to deliver what you're looking for.

Now that you've got a clear picture about what you can do to sell lots of books, let's turn our attention to helping you engage lots of new business with your book ...

— 10 —

YOU MUST MARKET WITH YOUR BOOK

A book is a wonderful way to raise your profile, build your brand, develop relationships with peers and potential customers, and ultimately sell more of your services.

—HONORÉE CORDER

The main reasons any businessperson writes a book are to increase visibility, book more business, and make more money. Your book can become your main business marketing tool, and while there are countless ways to market with your book, here I've included my favorite (and dare I say, most effective) strategies just for you and your book.

Best "Marketing with My Book" Strategies

A subtle difference from book marketing strategies, this particular set of suggestions centers solely on using your book to find new clients or engage new business. While some clients may come to you through the purchase of your book, many others can come in the most expeditious fashion through receiving your book as a gift (from you or someone else).

Yes, marketing with your book means you're going to give a lot of books away. Much in the same way that, up to now, you've been giving away your business card or handing out those awful folders full of information. If other people are anything like me, and they are, eventually those folders get thrown away without my ever reading them.

Typically, a book in the hands of a prospect will get the time and attention it deserves. Especially if you could be the person someone might hire to solve a problem they have (particularly a large or pressing problem), your book will get at least a cursory read, if not an in-depth look.

HAVE A BOOK HANDY, ALWAYS.

Keep a book on or near you at all times. Because the cost of a printed book is incredibly low, you can give your books away as easily as you would a business card. I tend to keep one of each of my books in easy-to-reach places. You can keep several books in your briefcase or purse, or in your desk, as well as a box in the backseat or trunk of your car, making it easy to grab one prior to each lunch or coffee appointment, networking event, or presentation.

When I receive a shipment of my books, I take a few minute to get organized so I always have them handy. Here are three tricks I've uncovered: (1) Take the time to autograph all your books. (2) Place a business card inside the front cover. (3) Keep manila envelopes and labels handy so you can quickly mail a book upon request.

SPEAKING OF THE MAIL ...

If you find yourself without a book, make it the topic of conversation. *I have a book you might like ...* My fallback plan is to get the person's mailing address and send them a signed book. Be sure to follow-up in a week or two to ensure they've received it. Your call or email will serve as a gentle nudge for them to read the book.

GIVE THAT PUPPY AWAY LIKE IT'S CANDY.

Most likely, your book won't have a hard cost of more than $2-3, and if you buy in bulk, it can be less than $0.50 per book. I bought the original *Tall Order!* books for $0.80 apiece and had no problem giving them away. I also, still to this day, leave them on planes and in coffee shops (Starbucks has a newspaper basket *and* sometimes a lending library).

If you have a hard time with the concept of giving the book away, let me help you here: *What is the acquisition value of a new client?* In other words, how much is a new client worth to you, initially and over time? $100? $500? $50,000? More? Just as you don't think, *there goes $2* every time you hand out a business card, let go of thinking about how much it costs to give away a book and focus on your ROI.

As a business coach, giving away a $2 book many times resulted in the engagement of a $1,000 client and usually more clients who paid more money. Focus on your desired outcomes and goals, not the money you're spending to give your book away. Plus, you can write off all those books!

I'll circle back to my unique strategies for "seeding the market" in a moment. Before that, I want to help you give away lots of books in record time to expedite the process of getting all those new clients you're dreaming about.

SIGNING VS. AUTOGRAPHING

When you give the book to someone, ask them if they'd like it signed. Usually, they do (be sure to always have a Sharpie on hand, too)! Sometimes, they want it made out to someone else to give as a gift. Signing and autographing are different—an autograph is just your signature on the title page; signing is when you add a personal message from you to the (intended) recipient.

Tip: Have a standard phrase based upon your book's topic to use when signing your book, such as: *It's time to turn your Vision to Reality* or *Your divorce is your new beginning!* You can, if you want, combine your usual message with something personal, but it's best not to be at a loss for words when the time comes to sign a book.

FIRST AND FOREMOST, MAKE A LIST OF YOUR KEY BUSINESS CONTACTS.

You may have already made this list for your book launch, but if you have opted to solely use your book to develop more business you'll definitely need your master list of contacts. If you've read either *Vision to Reality* or my networking book, *Business Dating*, then you're well-acquainted with my networking tool, the 12x12™. (Get a two-chapter sample of *Business Dating* at HonoreeCorder.com/BusinessDating.)

The 12x12™ consists of the twelve most important categories of professionals who are your strategic partners (i.e., the people who have your target clients as their clients, but are not in competition with you). For example, business attorneys work well with financial advisors, CPAs, and insurance providers … and vice versa.

You will develop relationships with twelve people in each category. Those 144 people should receive the first 144 copies of your book.

SECOND, MAKE A LIST OF KEY PEOPLE YOU KNOW WHO AREN'T ON YOUR 12x12™.

Perhaps you're active in a church, or you belong to a BNI chapter, Chamber of Commerce, industry association, or Rotary Club (or all of the above). Each of the groups has a number of people who would benefit from reading, and yes sharing, your book. If you can meet with them in person, fantastic. Offer the gift of a physical copy of your book, and be sure to ask if they would prefer a digital copy. If the best way to get them a book is to mail it, then mail it and make it memorable when they receive it. Here's a great article from Kobo Books on how to do just that: http://tinyurl.com/MemorableBook (even though this is for a fiction book, the article includes great ideas you can apply to your nonfiction books).

I have sold many books by thinking outside the box and also by listening to what people suggested I do with my books.

For example, Michael Wysocki is a family attorney in North Texas. He was using *The Successful Single Mom* as a lead generator for his practice. He placed the books (with a business card tucked inside) in the Starbucks nearest to his office in Plano. Why? Because he knew women would meet their girlfriends for coffee to discuss their rocky relationships and upcoming divorces. A few high-ticket divorces found their way onto his docket using this strategy, and it can work for you in your business.

Good ideas can be found everywhere, and one needs to be ready to pounce when these gems present themselves. Practice paying attention so that you too can stumble upon something great.

Another family attorney who had been gifted a copy of *If Divorce is a Game, These are the Rules,* asked me if I would print a version of the book where the back cover was branded for her law firm. She was interested in having her logo and contact information on the back instead of my sales copy. (Sales copy is about why someone should buy the book, if you're gifting the book strictly to strategic partners and clients, sales copy can be replaced with firm or company information.) I didn't hesitate to say yes.

Being the publisher, as well as the author, has advantages, and I had the power to make those executive decisions. Why did I need sales copy on the back cover if she was going to buy the books solely for the purposes of growing her business? I didn't.

It took me less than a day to make the changes and place the order (and by me, I mean my assistant). In her initial order, the attorney bought 250 copies and has continued to order more copies a few times a year for the past few years as she has expanded her practice and brought on new attorneys.

This isn't the only custom deal I've done, but it was the first, and it opened up my mind to all the possibilities for making the decision to buy in bulk easier for the potential customer.

How could this apply to you? You could write a book that other professionals buy in bulk and use to promote their businesses. How many real estate agents have used Gary Keller's *The One Thing* to recruit and motivate their teams? (Answer: lots and lots!)

Do Seven Marketing Actions Every Day

As I mentioned, when I wrote my first book, I took Mark Victor Hansen's suggestion to do seven things every day to promote my business with my book. My thought was *What a great idea!* Not one to, at least initially, try to improve on a great idea, I wrote down the seven things he and Jack Canfield did every day and did them myself.

While *Tall Order!* was being printed, I got busy doing my seven daily book marketing activities. Now that was in 2004, so I can't begin to tell you what all seven were back then, but I do remember that one of them was "get featured in local newspapers and magazines." I was shocked when it worked—I was featured in *Las Vegas Magazine* and a couple of other local newspapers and publications, and I won't lie, it was pretty cool. Today, local magazines or newspapers don't exist in abundance, but you can find them and, with the right approach, get featured in them as well.

Twelve years later, I'm still taking at least seven marketing actions every day to sell books as well as find new readers and clients.

The printer I used to publish the original version of *Tall Order!* had a minimum print run of 250 books. But the cost per book decreased based upon the number of units, and the cost was a fraction of that if I ordered 5,000 instead. Being the fiscally responsible person I am, that is exactly what I did. Then I had a "holy shiznit" moment when I realized 5,000 books were going to show up on my doorstep in five to six weeks (which, as it turned out, was only 27 small-ish boxes and wasn't nearly the truck load I thought it would it would be). With visions of my third-car garage turned into a sad version of a storage unit, I knew I needed to get selling, and fast! Thus, I started hustling on the list of seven things to do.

But here's where it gets interesting (and awesome): because I was focusing on selling books and engaging new coaching and training clients in multiple ways every day, *I found them!* In fact, while the original order of 5,000 was in production, I sold 6,000 more copies. New problem: I didn't have enough books coming! Yes, I sold or gave away one copy here, one copy there, five and 10 copies here, and 25 copies there. But I also sold a few batches of one thousand copies and even received one order for 3,000 copies. The larger orders I sold at a discount, but I still grossed over $100,000 before I ever saw one book in person.

Now, I'm of a generation that thinks it's pretty gauche to brag or talk numbers. I know some people like to do income reports and brag about how much they are making, and that is just not my style. But I think it's important that I pull back the curtain just a little so that (a) you know I'm legit and (b) you are encouraged to make your list and get started right away.

Because of the initial and early results with my first book, fifty books later, I am constantly looking for new, unique, and effective ways to find new readers and sell more books. I don't do very much coaching or speaking anymore, but as I expand my catalog of books on a variety of topics (writing, business, success, divorce, single parents, and eventually fiction), I am perpetually looking for new ways to find readers.

Master List of Book Marketing & Client-Finding Strategies

I suggest you make a master list of all of the strategies you can find, and then one by one, a few at a time (or even 7 at a time) give them a try. Make sure you give them long enough to work (perhaps 100 days) and adjust them as the market changes or you notice they are working … or not.

Sometimes strategies take a while to bear fruit, and others you'll have to alter to fit your specific type of book. Some will work better with some books than others. Some will work for a while, and then become ineffective. Pay close attention to what is working, what isn't working, what is no longer working, and see if you can change or adjust them so they work well for you and your particular book.

Keep in mind that data is very important, and you will want to track it so you know for sure if a strategy is working for you or not. Keep track of the marketing strategies you're using and where your new clients and book sales are coming from. This will provide you with incontrovertible evidence.

Let's Get Ninja

A *ninja* was a covert agent or mercenary in feudal Japan. The functions of the ninja included espionage, sabotage, infiltration, assassination, and guerrilla warfare. Their covert methods of waging irregular warfare were deemed "dishonorable" and "beneath" the samurai caste, which observed strict rules about honor and combat.

My definition of a ninja is a little more fun (and definitely more honorable—no assassinations required) and still stealthy, and quite frankly, awesome!

Becoming a book selling and sharing ninja was the means of getting my book and information into the hands of as many people as possible, without spending a lot of unnecessary time, money, or energy. I wanted (and still want) maximum results with the smallest budget, least amount of effort, *and* in the fastest time possible.

When you sell or give away enough books, you increase the chances of clients organically flowing to you. What follows are some of my very favorite ninja-esque strategies for finding clients through book gifts and sales … and so much more.

GIVE BOOKS AWAY.

As I've mentioned, once you are an author, I believe the number one way for someone to discover you is through your book ... because someone else recommends or gives your book to a colleague, client, or friend. To that end, I suggest giving away as many books as you can, as fast as you can, and as soon as you can. *Tall Order!* is now 14 years old, but if you haven't heard about it before now, the book is new to you. Even a book that's been around 100 years is new to the person who hasn't heard about it yet. If you have the opportunity to give someone a book, by all means *give them your book!* The hard costs of sponsoring luncheons, buying ads, or even treating someone to lunch or coffee can add up quickly and pale in comparison to the gift of a book.

And, none of those other marketing strategies even come close to the maximum coolness of a book.

In the case of my original *Tall Order!* (2004 version), I purchased those first 5,000 copies for $4,000, a cost of $0.80 per book. If you're new or just starting out, spending even a few dollars over and over might be too much for your pocketbook to bear. I get it—I'm fiscally responsible, remember? I think any and every business should be revenue positive. And make no mistake, your book is not just a book, it is a business! At the very least it can and should be a positive revenue stream to your overall business.

Keep in mind you can order between 1-999 copies of your book through Amazon's KDP. The cost is based upon the number of pages and size of the book. This book will cost around $2, which is far less than my initial hard cost of $4,000 just for the printing of my first book.

You can also use BookFunnel to give away free copies of your ebook anytime you'd like. Running a quarterly free book promotion is never a bad idea, and Amazon offers that option as well (if your book is enrolled in KDP Select).

STRATEGIC PARTNER GIFTS.

Each occupant of your 12x12™, otherwise known as the master list of people with whom you network in an effort to exchange referrals, can give away your book. In addition, there are multiple options for how they can distribute your book. Here are two:

They can give away copies of your book to their clients to promote their business. A book as a gift says, *I'm thinking about you and what you might need*, so this gift will serve to raise their own standing with their clients.

Your strategic partners can give your book to their clients and strategic partners to help you promote your business. Imagine you're a divorce attorney. If an estate planning attorney gives a divorcing woman a copy of *The Divorced Phoenix* with your card inside, it could mean a new client for you and a better quality relationship for them.

CUSTOM PRINTED BOOKS.

Remember family attorney Michael Wysocki? He was the first person to ask me if he could customize the back cover of *The Successful Single Mom* using his firm's logo, description, and contact information.

One of the beauties of custom printed books (and oh, is there so much beauty!) is the fact that people buy your book in bulk. My preferred printer's minimum print run is 250 books, and they can handle increments of 500 up to 10,000. My clients can order the books, pay me directly, and I can have the books shipped to them. The work on my end is strictly administrative. You can charge a wholesale price for the book and still, because of volume, pocket a tidy profit.

I share this tip, though a lot of strategy is required to put together an effective plan to sell custom printed books. You must understand the sales process and gain clarity about the type of client who purchases books (instead of writing their own) to use as a marketing tool. I want to open my playbook to you, but you need to understand that this is advanced stuff and requires strategic and tactical thinking.

For example, several of my clients throughout the years have successfully used other authors' books to promote their businesses, and still others are now using their own books to generate new business, as well as sell in bulk to earn an additional revenue stream.

So, I share this as a small, but not exactly simple example. Still, if this tactic seems right up your alley, and you want to learn more, write to my assistant at Assistant@HonoreeCorder.com (or visit HonoreeCorder.com/Coaching so we can discuss whether my intensive ninja book coaching is right for you).

Note: When you get to the point where you need to order more than 10,000 copies, a high print run printer is your best bet.

Advanced Ninja

In addition to using printed books, there are a few additional low-cost ways to gain exposure for your book that cut the cost to a fraction of the cost of an entire book (even at $2):

Use Postcards.

When I published *Vision to Reality* in 2013, I had postcards made with the book cover on the front (visit HonoreeCorder.com/YouMustBonuses to see it). This enabled me to send a postcard and ask the recipient if they would like a copy of the book. They had the option of using the QR code on the message side of the postcard to purchase the eBook, paperback, or audiobook directly from Amazon, or they could visit my website (also listed) to purchase a signed copy from me. The cool thing about postcards is that anyone who sees the postcard could be intrigued enough to look up the book and get a copy if it was right for them.

Since then, I have had postcards made for *If Divorce Is a Game, These are the Rules*. My assistant sends out a few a week to divorce attorneys with the message "To request a complimentary copy, email Assistant@HonoreeCorder.com, and we'll be happy to send you one." The postcard is a low cost and effective way to raise awareness about the book and has produced another fun result: large quantity purchases and even custom printed copies.

BOOKMARKS ARE AWESOME, TOO.

For *The Successful Single Mom* and *The Successful Single Dad* books, I created bookmarks that could be shipped along with the original printed copies of the book. Because the book predated CreateSpace, I had purchased thousands of copies and distributed them on Amazon through their Amazon Advantage program (https://affiliate-program.amazon.com). But as luck would have it, I not only changed addresses, I also got married, changed my name, and moved to another state … which made the contact information and even website listed inside the book null and void.

Rather than create the world's largest book bonfire, I decided to get creative and figure out a way to update the info without wasting the book. I inserted bookmarks inside the front cover with a QR code and a special offer, which enabled me to sell the books. Bookmarks can also be mailed, left in strategic places, and even used in giveaways.

Both postcards and bookmarks are incredibly cheap. Postcards run about $150 for 2500, and it takes quite a while to give away 2500 postcards, even with fierce intention and determination!

Bookmarks are equally as inexpensive—you'll have to give away many to spend even a penny.

STAMPS.

I recently bought stamps for several of my books, including this book, *Prosperity for Writers, Business Dating, The Successful Single Mom,* and *Vision to Reality*. They are the full front covers of the books, made thumbnail size and in stamp form—the cost is a tiny bit more than that for standard first-class postage to cover the printing. I get compliments on them every time I use them, and again, they aren't limited to the intended recipient's eyeballs. Anyone who sees them will take notice because they are different. You can get yours from USPS.com. These stamps also make great gifts for authors. I've posted them several times on my Instagram feed, which you can find at Instagram.com/Honoree.

SEEDING THE MARKET.

Giving away books, specifically leaving them in easy to find places, is what I call "seeding the market." I mentioned earlier that I seed the market by leaving my books, postcards, and bookmarks pretty much everywhere I go. I know this works because of all the times someone has stumbled upon my book, read it, and gotten in touch.

I've had several people discover something I've left behind, send me an email, subscribe to my list, and even hire me. More than two or three *dozen* times. My favorite emails are the ones from someone telling me they stumbled upon my book just when they needed it most.

You can even read a testimonial here (http://tinyurl.com/BDTestimonial) from someone who discovered one of my books at my local carwash!

Am I making money directly from the books and postcards I leave behind or send? Not necessarily, yet that's not the idea behind this strategy. Is it possible, probable even, that the person who finds the book might purchase another book, one of my courses? Or hire me as their coach or a speaker for one of their events? Or even buy an ebook copy of the book they found? *Yes.* All of the above has happened, making my seeding strategy incredibly effective. Here are just a few of the places I leave them:

DOCTORS AND DENTISTS OFFICES.

At least once a year, my doctor tasks me with having my blood tested. So I leave my books in his office and at the clinic. My husband and daughter also find themselves in doctors' offices (and dentists and massage therapists and nail salons) at various times throughout the year. You can bet your sweet self that books, bookmarks, and postcards are left behind each and every time.

STARBUCKS COFFEE SHOPS.

Starbucks provide their very own unique and wonderful opportunity for you. Not only can you write there, and have snacks and drinks at your disposal, you can meet clients, increase your discoverability, and find new readers! As I mentioned earlier, each Starbucks has either a lending library or a newspaper basket—or both. When someone is finished with their newspaper, it can be left behind for the next person or placed in the basket near the "newspapers for sale" rack for reuse. Well, who said only newspapers go in those baskets? Not me! I don't visit a Starbucks anywhere on my travels (even if it is to one of the two locations that are less than three minutes from my home) that I don't leave at least one of my books behind. On the rare occasion I don't have a book handy, I will add a postcard or a bookmark to the information board. My local Starbucks loves me for it (and they always have a Venti

Americano, or Youthberry tea with three Splenda packets at the ready when they see me coming).

I have gotten five new subscribers to my list in the past week from Baton Rouge, Louisiana ... one of the places I stopped going and returning on a recent trip with my family. Coincidence? Who knows, but I don't think so.

My family and I like to travel. On one particular day, we were in Miramar Beach, Florida. I like to have a hot tea in the morning (and some Gruene Coffee Haus Texas Pecan, if I'm home). My husband is more of a chai latté drinker, and my daughter is obsessed with the "pink drink," so Starbucks is a place we can all find what we need. After we had finished our first meal of the day at a local breakfast stop, paid, and made the lengthy walk to the car (easily over twenty feet from the front door) someone suggested we find a Starbucks. As usual, without objection, the motion was passed.

The thing about writing a book that's designed to help people is that there is as much mental prosperity as there is financial, and some days more.

Sure, it's nice to find a new reader and put a ducket or two in the old retirement account, but ultimately the biggest rush is being the answer when someone desperately needs it.

Such was the case at Starbucks (such is usually the case at Starbucks!). One of the baristas was a delightful woman whom I shall call Julie. Julie is a single mother of two children ages eight and ten.

She seemed exhausted. I've been there, and being a solo parent can be, in and of itself, exhausting. Fortunately, I've also written several books on the subject, and with only slightly less flair than a Las Vegas magician, I produced a copy and gave it to her.

You could tell by the look on her face it was exactly what she needed. She thanked me profusely, and I noticed before we left that she was sneaking a peak at her new book by the espresso machine.

Will Julie become a lifelong reader? I have no idea. She may buy another book, or possibly give it to a friend, or even find it isn't for her. She might read it and then leave it on the table at Starbucks to be found by the next single mother in need. Regardless, by having the book handy as a part of my daily routine, I'm ready to help when the need arises.

And that is enough, but it may also lead to a rabid reader who tells *everyone* about my book on Facebook—that has happened too.

About two years ago, I sent a box of *The Successful Single Mom* (box count: 128) with my in-laws when they left on a 15-state tour. On this trip, they drove to Nova Scotia and back … leaving my books at Starbucks all along the way. A win for Starbucks (repeat customers!), a win for the customers (buy a coffee, get a book!), and a win for me. New readers in new places have been exposed to me and my book with a relatively small time and money investment.

AIRPORTS AND AIRPLANES.

As my husband and daughter are always up for an adventure, we travel as much as we can. Whether we drive or fly, I'm provided with even more opportunities (as are you) to seed the market. Leave a book in the seatback pocket, a postcard in the airline magazine, a bookmark in a book similar to yours in the airport bookstore, and any of the above in any seat you use along the way.

BOOKSTORES.

Speaking of bookstores ... until Amazon recently opened bookstore number one in Seattle to showcase its best-selling titles (congratulations to my business partner in *The Miracle Morning* book series, Hal Elrod, for being one of the featured!), I was convinced brick and mortar bookstores were not long for this world. Now, I'm not so sure. But what I have been doing for years, because I have never been "one of the chosen few" whose books were distributed to bookstores everywhere, is put my books in bookstores exactly where they would be on the shelf if they *were*. Just one copy. Spine out ... I mean, I'm not paying for the front cover facing space. (Big grin.)

When I go back a couple of days later, you know what? Nine times out of ten, the book *is not there*. So either someone found it and tried to buy it, or someone at the store found it, and well, I don't know what exactly. But on dozens of occasions, I have received a call from bookstores as small as the mom and pop independent store in Milwaukee, Wisconsin to the Barnes and Noble I can hit with a rock from my front door wanting to know how they can get more books.

Note: I wouldn't recommend going to the same bookstore on a regular basis until you get an order.

MY FAMILY AND FRIENDS ARE PART OF MY MARKETING TEAM.

My husband, Byron, had an office at We Work (a co-op workspace where he rented and shared common areas with other renters) for about a year,. A few times a week, he would leave any or all of my business books in the common areas, conference rooms, and the private phone booths for the next user to find. He also left behind postcards and bookmarks at his regular Starbucks.

Now we are based in Nashville and also always on the move, so we use various coffee shops in the places we're staying as our offices. Of course we leave books there, and sometimes there are even retail opportunities (many mom and pop coffee shops sell merchandise other than food and are happy to co-op my books).

A few of my friends travel quite a bit for work, and for those who are (not yet) authors, I give them a book or two and some postcards to help me with my cause. I have friends all over the world, and they are cool enough to help me get the word out about my books (on and offline). I bet your friends and family would be delighted to do the same.

A Fantastic Ninja Idea

J.A. Huss, one of my author friends and someone who prolifically writes romance books, held a contest and asked her readers to change their Facebook photo to the cover image of her book. J.A. has thousands of fans, and the number of people who heard about her book because they saw a temporary profile photo, yielded thousands of additional sales. Imagine having even twenty people change their image to the cover of your book, which their thousands of collective friends and connections will see. Cool, right?

Think Like a Ninja

I want you to think like a ninja when it comes to using your book to grow your business. I didn't originate thinking like a ninja, I learned it from other ninjas who were doing things I hadn't thought of until I heard their ideas. I believe you can take any idea you hear and improve upon it.

Claudia Azula Altucher wrote a great book called *Become an Idea Machine*, which I know you would derive inspiration from reading. In this book, she encourages her readers to brainstorm ten new ideas a day, new ideas for anything and everything that's important. Imagine brainstorming ten new marketing ideas for your book every day. Of course, they won't all be home runs, but if even one of your ideas works wonders, won't you be stoked by the results and, ultimately, the increase in your bottom line? I know you will.

You've learned about marketing your book. You've learned about marketing with your book. Now ...

The Time Has Come

The purpose of this book is not only to give you a whole bunch of ideas. My purpose is to give you a whole bunch of ideas that you *use*, ideas that create a spark and birth other ideas—all of which you deploy with great success, starting with writing your book. If I have done my job well, I've inspired you to write, publish, and market your book with great ideas. Perhaps these same ideas have done a Vulcan mind meld with some of your ideas, spawning new and even better ideas ... culminating in the massive growth of your book sales, business, and brand.

Hopefully, you have been inspired and have already started penciling in some ninja secrets that, when you share them with me, will cause me to exclaim, "That is genius!"

The best part about ideas is that, once they start coming, they come fast and furious. They won't all be gold-star gems of brilliance, and that's okay. Because you've taken the time to add intention and purpose to your direction, you'll be able to sort through your ideas and be able to choose the best ones for you to use right now.

I have shared with you my favorites, and now I'm putting on my coaching hat with the goal of getting you into action. Before you read any further, grab a pen and some paper or start a new Evernote document, and begin to craft a "finding readers plan." Write down the ideas that struck you as solid and appropriate for you and add them to your action plan.

Even while your book is still in the pre-production stage, I want you to find and attract new clients as soon as tomorrow (or even today!), so let's hurry up and get your plan in place. Identify the ninja ideas you think will work best and get on the road to finding readers fast.

One Last Thing to Keep in Mind

TEMPER YOUR EXPECTATIONS.

Wouldn't it be wonderful if you gave someone your book and they called you three hours later and told you how great it was? Yeah, so that's never going to happen. It is overly optimistic to expect someone to have read your book the day after receiving it. I have books I purchased over a year ago that I haven't had a chance to read quite yet. Remember that you are asking people to give you at least an hour, and potentially hours, of their most precious resource: their time. I consider it a huge honor when someone spends their time reading my book. Give your readers some space before asking them if they've read your book (but do ask, a gentle nudge never hurt anyone).

Oh yes, and thank *you* for reading this book!

– 11 –

YOU'RE IN GREAT COMPANY

*Start writing, no matter what.
The water does not flow until the faucet is turned on.*

—LOUIS L'AMOUR

I used to think all authors were old (or dead), highly successful professionals, or professional writers. If I held their book in my hands, I assumed they were too many levels above me to fathom or achieve. I was right and wrong.

Some of my favorite writers were either dead or incredibly successful and still alive, in the cases respectively of Napoleon Hill (*Think and Grow Rich*) and Tony Robbins (*Awaken the Giant Within*).

What was cool for me to realize was that a number of the people I had come to admire through reading their books were ordinary people, just like me, who happened to have written a book.

The first big-time author I met in person was Tony Robbins. A magnetic and giant person, Tony changed my life first through his books *Unlimited Power* and *Awaken the Giant Within*, then through his *Personal Power* audio program, and eventually through his seminars. Purchasing *Awaken the Giant Within* for $12 in 1992 was perhaps one of the best things I've ever done. My lifetime value to Tony, coming to his work through his book, has been tens of thousands of dollars, as I have attended every single one of his seminars (some multiple times, and even with my husband), listened to (and still own) every audio program, and read and given away all of his books. To this day, if Tony does something new, I usually want to know about it and buy it.

The next author I met and got to know personally is Jeffrey Gitomer. I first read his column in the *Pacific Business Journal* (the business newspaper in Honolulu), and then read *The Little Red Book of Sales*. A friend introduced us after I had moved to Las Vegas, and it was Jeffrey who helped me tighten my book writing and publishing game as well as encouraged me to keep writing.

Today, I know lots of authors, many of whom credit becoming an author with much, if not all, of the personal and professional success they enjoy today. Who else has written a book and catapulted their careers to where it is today? Many, many people, and hopefully there's at least one who will serve as inspiration and encouragement for you.

Before I share the thoughts of a few authors I know personally, I want you to know that becoming a famous or well-known author doesn't have to be one of your intended outcomes. There are tens of thousands of authors, self-published indeed, who have used their book to grow their businesses. Not only have you not heard of them, you never will. They have used their book to grow their business, practice, or organization without gaining any national notoriety.

I believe this is important to note because, while you may know some or all of the authors mentioned in this book, becoming a recognizable figure might not be what you want from publishing your book. And that's just fine, indeed.

Co-host of the *Sell More Books Show*, Bryan Cohen is a self-published and full-time author of both fiction and nonfiction (*Ted Saves the World, 1001 Creative Writing Prompts,* and *How to Work for Yourself* to name just a few). Bryan began self-publishing on Amazon after realizing that he needed another way to earn income online, one that truly compensated him for his effort.

Initially he published a book on his website and earned about $100. Then someone gave him a tip to try publishing on Amazon's KDP platform. Bryan had no insight about pricing, formatting, or the importance of a terrific cover. Still, he has become a successful author.

> *I could put my book in the biggest marketplace in the entire world, that was amazing to me! My first month, instead of $100, I sold 100 books at $2.99 and made just over $200. That was all I needed to keep going, and eventually I built up my book so it was #1 in its category for an entire year. I sold 20 copies of* 1000 Creative Writing Prompts *a day in 2011. It was so amazing, I ended up writing sequels, workbooks, and so much more. This month (June 2016), I've sold 400 workbooks alone.*
>
> *It's been amazing for me! I think the greatest thing about publishing on Amazon (or any other online platform) is the opportunity to reach people you never would have found on your own. A blog, class, or workshops or trainings—in any of these settings, you certainly do reach and connect with a lot of people. A lot of people in business have products that cost $500, $1,000, or more. These are sold through the great relationships you build with your clients. A book is at a smaller price point, and it allows you to connect with potentially tens of thousands of people you never could have connected with otherwise. A book is one of the best ways to build a brand I've ever seen. Your cover is out there, and it's representing you, even people who don't buy your books get to see you, your brand, and your niche. You are simultaneously selling thousands*

upon thousands of copies while many more people are seeing your brand and paying to see it!

It's like getting paid for your own advertising. How often does that happen?

Self-publishing on Amazon has made a huge difference at showing I am an expert in my subject area. If anyone were to question my expertise as a SME or teacher or taking my course, they could easily go on Amazon and see just how many books I have and how many reviews I have.

You can learn more about Bryan Cohen at BestPageForward.net.

I had the pleasure of working with Pat Petrini, creator of the Real Estate Shortcut (www.RealEstateShortcut.com, on *The Miracle Morning for Network Marketers* (www.TMMforNetworkMarketers.com), which became an instant #1 best seller and helped him reach several of his professional goals in one fell swoop.

Writing a book has had significant impact for me both professionally and personally. On a professional level, not only has the book itself been a significant income stream, but it has dramatically expanded my audience as well as taken my credibility within my niche to an entirely new level, both of which have led directly to significantly increased revenue streams.

On a personal level, the act of writing the book forced me to practice "deep work" (long periods of undistracted mental focus) on a level that I probably haven't done since college. It reminded me of what can be accomplished with this kind of focused effort. Additionally, writing comes much more naturally to me now, and it has opened up a whole new outlet for my ideas and creativity.

If one of your goals, even if it is yet unspoken, is to write full-time, know this: it is possible! Several of the authors in this book began by writing their first book and never imagined it would open the door to many other incredible opportunities. I did not foresee a daily writing habit and several books per year when I wrote *Tall Order!* It never occurred to me I could earn a full-time living from writing, and I certainly did not imagine I would write fiction! And it's not just me who has discovered a new life path through the power of the self-published book.

While today she mainly writes fiction, *New York Times* bestselling author Julie Huss, (who writes under the pen name J.A. Huss) made a comment on Facebook I thought was a perfect fit for this book.

> *In fact, if I had not quit that biotech program and finished my graduate studies in forensic toxicology, I would've never written my first book, which was forensic science for high school kids. And if I had never written that, I would've never written all of the hundreds of other nonfiction books, which means I would've never written my first fiction book a few years later. I think it all worked out.*

Worked out indeed. Julie is now a full-time writer and bestselling author who writes and publishes several books each year. But she's not alone.

Barrie Davenport, author of multiple books and cofounder of the self-publishing site Authority.Pub has seen a dramatic increase in her income, which stems from her decision to write just one book and led to many books.

> *Without question, self-publishing has changed the trajectory of my business. I'm a certified coach and personal development blogger, and when I first launched my business several years ago, I was challenged (nicely) by author, speaker, and mega coach Steve Chandler to write a book. I wrote my first book,* The 52-Week Life Passion Project, *as a result, and having a book published definitely added to my authority and name recognition in the personal development industry and brought in some additional income. It wasn't until I met Steve Scott, one of the most prolific*

and successful self-published authors out there, that I saw the financial potential for self-publishing a catalog of books. He mentored me in the process, and as of today, I have published 11 self-improvement books and partner with Steve on a successful self-publishing course called Authority Pub Academy and host a related podcast, Authority Self-Publishing. *All of this happened as a result of taking action on that first book. Self-publishing can lead to a variety of other income streams and business opportunities that one might not anticipate when they first consider writing a book.*

Speaking of Steve Scott, Hal and I had the pleasure of publishing *The Miracle Morning for Writers* with him in 2016. I first learned about Steve when I listened to him on *The James Altucher Show* (here's the episode on YouTube: http://tinyurl.com/AltucherShow). That one interview blew my mind and left me inspired and encouraged to write more books. Because Steve had, at the time, published about forty-one books and was earning $40,000 per month. I don't care who you are, that's real money!

I had set a goal a couple of years prior to create an additional stream of income from my books that was enough to live on. Steve and James's interview gave me incontrovertible proof I could do it. (Note: if Steve, James, and I can do it, you can also do it!) I'm sure you can imagine my delight when Hal suggested we write a Miracle Morning book with Steve and ask James to do the Foreword. I went from listening to that one interview to having the opportunity to know the people I had admired from afar. Yet another power of a self-published book: the ability to connect with people you think are super cool!

Here's what Steve had to say about self-publishing.

I have been an online entrepreneur for over 12 years, which means I've tried a variety of business models throughout my career. I have found that writing books has been—hands down—the BEST decision I have ever made. The advantage of writing books is you get to sell DIRECTLY to an audience (without the hassle of having to build a platform ahead of time). If a reader likes your book hook, then all she has to do is click the "buy" button, and then you have another customer.

On a personal level, self-publishing has changed my life in a number of ways: (1) I get to build a community JUST from people who like my content. (2) I generate a reliable full-time income from book sales alone (and have done so since early 2013). (3) I have been interviewed and quoted on many popular podcasts and blogs. (4) I have made a number of amazing connections with great authors who I also admire (like Honorée).

Overall, I feel that writing books has been singularly the BEST business decision that I've ever made!

The aforementioned entrepreneur, podcaster, prolific writer and best-selling author, James Altucher shared that he didn't want to write a business book or nonfiction; he wanted to write novels. His first goal has remained a guiding light: always get better as a writer. He ended up writing a bunch of hardcore business books, including *Choose Yourself,* which remained in the top 100 nonfiction books on Amazon for about two years. The topic of choosing one's self is where James was most interested, especially because "there isn't enough validation to go around anymore, you have to be comfortable validating yourself and feel good about that and yourself."

When it came time to decide between traditional and self-publishing, James had a great answer.

Self-publish! Of course, because I am going to Choose Myself! It was the best decision I could make, and it's changed, enhanced, and grown my life in ways I can't begin to explain.

And last, but certainly not least, Kevin Tumlinson, author of *30-Day Author* spoke about how becoming an author changed his life.

> *I wrote a nonfiction book, and my life will never be the same because it gives me a touch point for interacting with the community I serve. It's a shortcut to establishing my authority on the topic of writing and publishing. But the bigger benefit has come in the relationships that have formed because readers enjoyed the book and found it useful, and shared it with their friends. I've made business contacts, I've been engaged to speak, I've gotten new clients, and I've been invited to numerous interviews because of the book. And I've had readers contact me to tell me that the book changed at least some aspect of their lives for the better—the greatest honor I can think of!*

As you can see, when you self-publish your first book, you will be in great company.

There are two final thoughts I want to leave you with: First, to a person, not one single author I talked to regrets the time, money, and effort it took to write their book. There is something delightful about becoming an author and signing your book for people, and every author I spoke with regrets only that they didn't start writing their book sooner; and second, there is absolutely no way to predict the incredible opportunities that will stem from your book. The people you will meet, the places you will go, the lives you will touch, and perhaps the business you'll receive is, without question, unlimited.

— 12 —

YOU MUST WRITE A BOOK AND YOU MUST GET STARTED NOW

*Do not wait; the time will never be "just right."
Start with where you stand, and work with whatever
tools you have at your command, and better tools
will be found as you go along.*
—GEORGE HERBERT

If you're anything like me, you've already come up with a few book ideas and perhaps even started working your way through the steps I've outlined. But perhaps you're still cogitating about whether you should really write a book *now* and, if so, the best course of action to take, and when you might be able to fit writing a book into your schedule.

Let me address each of those, because I understand any hesitation you might have … I mean, you're using all twenty-four hours of every single day already. You might not have dozens of years of experience under your belt and think you might not be the least bit qualified to write a book. And, of course, I know you don't want to dedicate what could be hundreds of hours of time as well as money to a project that might not succeed.

I get it, I really do. I write this with total passion and without any hesitation and with all the enthusiasm and gusto I can muster: I believe *you must write a book* … and *you must start immediately*. To help you close the loop and commit to writing a book, I'm going to address what I believe to be your main reservations.

"I'M NOT READY YET."

Your years of experience, or lack thereof, might not matter as much as you think. Even my clients with more than thirty years of experience, when we first discuss the possibility of writing a book, have a hard time with the concept that they would have enough knowledge or insight to fill an entire book. You might be amused, as I am, to know that once they start writing, they talk about their book as "their first book." It doesn't take long for the book bug to bite and for them to find the inspiration for more books. I didn't think I would write a second book, or a third, or a tenth. But the same has been true for me: just when I think I'm all out of ideas and that the book I'm writing is *definitely* going to be my last, well, either I find inspiration or someone hands it to me.

If you're still new to the line of work you're in, or you're in your very first line of work, you could surmise you don't have enough to say. You know more than you think you know, and have more to offer than you might imagine.

Let's consider Napoleon Hill, author of *Think & Grow Rich*. Napoleon Hill was neither old nor wealthy when he set out to interview those who had both age and money. He combined his experience with his desire for knowledge, and *Think & Grow Rich* had sold more than 70 million copies by 2011, and is ranked by *BusinessWeek Magazine*, the sixth best-selling business paperback of all time. Some might argue he had no business writing such a book, but I for one, am glad he did. That book, and much of his other work, has enriched my life in so many ways.

Combining your knowledge and experience with the knowledge and experience of others can be gold (literally and figuratively).

If you have, or have had, a challenge, others have it too. People are alike, and where a problem exists in my life, chances are you or someone you know has had the same problem. I need the benefit of your experience and knowledge, and very often the only way I'm going to get access to it is through your book.

CRAFT YOUR BOOK IDEA.

The fastest and easiest way to come to a decision regarding the topic of your book is to think in terms of "problems" (or inquiries) and "solutions." First, jot down a list of common problems many (if not all) of your clients have. I'm sure you've found yourself giving the same advice over and over again (I know I have, especially around this particular topic of writing a book). If there are ten individuals who have the same problem, chances are there are many, many more.

I like to write the problems in the form of questions, such as *Should I write a book?* And *What's the best way to launch my book?* Just as I know the answers to these questions, you already know the answers to the questions posed to you by your prospective and current clients.

Even a neophyte has accumulated enough knowledge to be in business, and chances are you're giving the same advice to different people. I believe you can, and should, make your knowledge available in (you guessed it) a book.

Now take the questions and answer them. Note how you advise your clients about their various problems and the solutions you provide—write it all down. This, very simply, is the meat of your book. If it would be helpful, record yourself as you're giving advice. Have the audio transcribed or use the recording yourself to help you get the words on paper.

If you provide advice that is particularly specific in nature, or writing down advice could get you or the person reading your book in hot water (i.e., specific legal or financial advice), be sure to speak in general terms, or use specific examples (protecting confidentiality, of course), and use disclaimers. The reason I have been hired to work with individuals is the same reason you've been hired to work with individuals: about 80–95 percent of the advice we both give is applicable to just about everyone. It's that last 5–20 percent of a person's situation that makes them special and why they need our brains on what they are doing.

Your book is meant to be a guide, not the full enchilada. Your book will give one-size-fits-all advice that is helpful and provides great direction for your avatar (and of course, others as well). Ultimately, you're the specialist with the information someone needs, and your book just might be what they need to hire you. Or, your book might be enough to give them everything they need. Your reader gets to decide, and either way, you've made a huge difference by providing your knowledge in an easily digestible format they can consume at their convenience.

Lest you think your perspective has been covered before, and well, by someone else, consider this: the way you share your perspective can be what allows someone to hear and benefit from it. Consider this Amazon review for my book, *Prosperity for Writers*, from Aurora:

I came upon this by accident and didn't expect to learn anything new about the way I think—in that I've read a lot of self-help books about changing one's world and how to keep your eyes on the positive. I wanted to read this, however, simply because it was geared toward writers. I loved it. I was so surprised at the fact there were new ideas in it. Sure, there were the old standbys about changing your world by changing how you think, but the fact it was geared toward writers and had a specific game plan on HOW to change your thinking was what really made it worthwhile and different.

Suze Orman, the infamous financial advisor, has written countless books on personal finances. She's written a book on just about every financial topic imaginable. But the books Suze authored didn't stop Robert Kiyosaki or Dave Ramsey from writing their own books. Suze, Robert, and Dave all tackle precisely the same topic, but from different perspectives and angles, each one infused with their personality and knowledge.

Your book might not be the first book on a topic, but it will be the first one you've written. It just might be, no it will be, just what your readers need to avoid disaster or gain something they really want.

And while all three of them have been well-known in the world, I would bet the first book each of them wrote was simply designed to help them get more business (not to develop a huge brand and get their own Sirius XM podcast).

"I DON'T HAVE THE TIME."

Everyone has the same twenty-four hours in a day, and some of us manage to write books during that time. Does it mean we give up something else? Sure. Is it worth it? You know I think it is! When you commit to writing your book, you'll be surprised how much time you can carve out to write it (or help your ghostwriter).

As I mentioned earlier, I write for an hour every morning. The consistency of my writing habit isn't always fun or easy, but

I consistently crank out around a thousand words a day, for an average of 30,000 words a month, and 360,000 words per year. No matter how you slice it, I am able to write several books a year simply on the production of those thousand words a day.

You can do the same, although you might not want to, or be able to, write first thing in the morning. You might want something a little more digestible to start. I suggest the following schedule for writing your book, using my "100 days of writing and 6 months to your book" structure as your model:

Timeline:

: Final First Draft Outline Due (2 days)

: First Rough Draft Due (allow 21 days)

: Final First Draft Due (allow 14 days)

: Send book to editor 1 (allow 8 days)

: Review edits (allow 1 day)

: Send book to proofreader (allow 4 days)

: Send book to formatter (allow 10 business days)

: Book to Street Team (2-3 weeks prior to Soft Launch)

: Soft launch (Friday before Hard Launch)

: Hard launch (Monday or Tuesday)

: Book party

Note: With this schedule, you'll need to schedule your editor and proofreader as soon as your outline is finished. This goes for your cover designer and interior layout designer as well. Any great editor/editing and design team will have limited availability of their schedule.

BEFORE YOU BEGIN ...

Come up with your working title, craft an outline, and schedule your writing session for days one through seven. Also, determine the date six months from your first writing day, and that's your launch date.

Side note: It is entirely possible there is an ideal date to launch your book. It's perfectly fine if that date is after the six-month goal (If it isn't, reconsider your ability to produce a book in less than six months without some external support). You can see this production schedule and a few more in *I Must Write My Book: The Companion Workbook to You Must Write a Book*.

SCHEDULE WRITING APPOINTMENTS.

Decide when you're going to write each day, and put it on your calendar. If regularly scheduled, same-time-every-day "appointments" won't work, put aside time for each day a week in advance.

Most of the time my schedule is predictable, but for those weeks when I'm traveling, on vacation, or there are other hiccups in my life, I have to make time to write on a case-by-case and day-by-day basis. Staying flexible and committed is your key to success when a predictable schedule is a dream and not a given.

SET A DAILY WRITING WORD COUNT GOAL.

Writing 500 words a day over the course of 100 days equals 50,000, more than enough for a good-sized nonfiction book. This leaves eighty days to put the finishing touches on your editing, formatting, sales and back cover copy, and cover design. Keep in mind, many of those extra steps can be accomplished while simultaneously writing your book. Curated with consistency, in six months, you will have a book.

KEEP GOING UNTIL IT'S DONE.

Just as you wouldn't put a time limit on a child learning how to walk or talk, it will serve you to keep going until your book is finished. Many authors report it took them several years to finish their first book. I'm not at all suggesting you give yourself a *forever* runway. I am a realist, however, and I know life happens. Publishing your book will take longer than you want it to, take more time, money, and effort than you'd like it to, and I can promise you one really cool thing: *it will all be worth it.* You won't regret giving it everything you have to in order to get it done; you will regret not making it happen sooner.

"WHAT IF IT FAILS?"

The only way your book can be deemed a failure is if you fail to write it. I hope you've taken my advice and set some strong goals for your book. I know beyond a shadow of a doubt your book will open doors for you that neither you nor I can know today.

You might miss your goals, spend too much money in the production of the book, and take time that could be used to build your business or spend time with your family. You might not make as much money as you'd like, either directly or indirectly from the book (at least at first). So what? The positives of having a book far outweigh any of these, I promise you.

I am of the strong opinion that writing a book will serve you more than you can possibly imagine, open doors that might otherwise have stayed locked, and connect you with clients and friends who might never had a way to find you before. And that's just the beginning!

Without my book series for single moms, I would never have connected and partnered with Hal Elrod, become a contributing blogger to the *Huffington Post*, or known some of the most amazing people I've had the pleasure to befriend.

Without my business books, I would still be *just* a coach and a speaker, charging far less than I am today for either or both of those services.

Without any of my books, I wouldn't be having this conversation with you today—encouraging you to write your book. The very book, I believe, that will change every aspect of your life.

Therefore, your book can only be a failure if you fail to write it.

Your Next Chapter

Your book begins a new chapter in your business life, and I hope you'll begin writing it today.

END OF BOOK STUFF

This book holds a special place in my heart because if I had never written a book, I wouldn't be living the life I'm living now. I can't imagine not knowing the great friends with whom I share amazing ideas and belly-laughs.

This is my first "end of book stuff" "chapter" … I'm borrowing this idea from my friend and fellow writer Julie Huss. I think it's a brilliant idea (you'll have to tell me if you agree) because sometimes there are things I want to say in a book that don't really have a place. Here are a couple from this book.

While it might seem that writing a book is only about the money, and the money is great, every book I've written is a personal journey of discovery. You might find, like I do, when you re-read what you've written you think, *this is actually good!* You have great things inside of you, and writing is the opportunity to get them out, share them with the world, help make the world a better place in some small way, *and* be creative all at the same time. I learn something new about myself with every book I write.

Also, I have always loved discovering new things I can do, and once I discovered how much I love writing, it was all I wanted to do. I mean, I could help lots of people! Coaching was something I did day in and day out (to the point where I would run out of words at the end of the day and not want to talk *at all*), and I helped people, but only a few at a time. Books connect me with people all over the world, and I love knowing my words are offering hope and ideas. Now that I'm not doing business coaching at all (I'm only helping a few aspiring authors to bring their books to life), I love writing more, and I'm even taking a crack at fiction. Stay tuned!

Lastly, every book gives me an idea for several more books. The main new idea from this book is to write about what happens beyond the book. I'm not sure what it means yet, what the idea will turn out to be (if anything), but I do know it's time to put the finishing touches on this one and get busy with the next one.

If you've read this far, I hope it means you have enjoyed this book and have already started on one of your own (my fingers and toes are seriously crossed over here!). Please send me an email, tell me what you think, and let's start a conversation about your book.

Happy writing, and thanks for reading!

THE TIME HAS COME.
BEGIN WRITING YOUR BOOK NOW!

"Before you set out to write your first book, there are a few things to think about. As we learn from Honorée, the best action plan for any book is planning to write it."

~Scott B. Allan, Author,
Relaunch Your Life

CAPTURE YOUR THOUGHTS, GAIN CLARITY, AND MOVE THROUGH THE PROCESS WITH EASE.

"Anyone who wants to validate their expertise needs to get the book and do the work. A book is your new business card. Highly recommend."

-Chris Syme, Author,
Sell More Books with Less Social Media

Quick Favor

I'm wondering, did you enjoy this book?

First of all, thank you for reading my book! May I ask a quick favor?

Will you take a moment to leave an honest review for this book on Amazon? Reviews are the BEST way to help others purchase the book.

You can go to the link below and write your thoughts. I appreciate you!

HonoreeCorder.com/YouMustReview

Gratitude

I give thanks for my husband and daughter, without whom I wouldn't laugh nearly as much or be living the coolest life ever.

My team is incredible: Alyssa, Dino, Adam … you all make me look so good! Thank you!

Finally, I give thanks for everyone who has ever read one of my books and said something nice about it. This book is for you. I hope your book brings you as much joy and as many blessings as my books have brought to me.

READY TO WRITE YOUR BOOK?

Crafting, writing, publishing, launching, and marketing a book is complex. With a simple process and an expert to answer your questions, you stand the best change of getting it done—and sooner than you think.

INDIE AUTHOR UNIVERSITY
presents
PUBLISHING PH.D. LIVE!

Learn how to **intentionally** craft the contents of your book and write it as quickly as possible.

Launch your book like a pro so that it sells forever online **and** offline..

Honorée Corder has guided dozens of authors to write, publish, and market their books to enhance their business. Learn how you can do the same!

JOIN THE NEXT COURSE TODAY

http://bit.ly/PubPhD

SPACES ARE LIMITED

Who is Honorée Corder

Honorée Corder is the author of dozens of books, including: *You Must Write a Book*; *I Must Write My Book*; *The Nifty 15: Write Your Book in Just 15 Minutes a Day!*; *The Prosperous Writers* book series; *Vision to Reality: How Short Term Massive Action Equals Long Term Maximum Results*; *Business Dating: Applying Relationship Rules in Business for Ultimate Success*; *The Successful Single Mom* book series; *If Divorce is a Game, These are the Rules*; and *The Divorced Phoenix*.

She is also Hal Elrod's business partner in *The Miracle Morning* book series, and together they've published fourteen titles to date. Honorée coaches business professionals, writers, and aspiring non-fiction authors who want to publish their books to bestseller status, create a platform, and develop multiple streams of income. She also does all sorts of other magical things, and her badassery is legendary. You can find out more at HonoreeCorder.com.

Honorée Enterprises, Inc.
Honoree@HonoreeCorder.com
http://www.HonoreeCorder.com
Twitter & Instagram: @Honoree
Facebook: http://www.facebook.com/Honoree

BOOK HONORÉE TO SPEAK

Honorée —you got me fired up! Thank you for building my confidence! Honorée's presentation was the perfect kick-off and her message of visualizing success was spot-on.
~Johnny B Truant, COO Sterling Stone

Honorée really captured the attention of our tribe, which is no easy task. Her quick-witted take on the world had them riveted—and keep in mind she followed Brooke Shields. Her stories are real, completely relatable, and just the sort of motivation women need to bring out their best.
~India Hicks, Founder, India Hicks Inc.

If you want engaging, results-oriented content without any fluff, I highly recommend booking Honorée Corder to speak at your event.
~Hal Elrod, Best-selling Author, *The Miracle Morning*

Honorée Corder is THE self-publishing expert, but that's not all. For almost 20 years she's inspired and guided professionals to double their income and triple their time off. Her genuine charm and expert knowledge are guaranteed to help your audience, business, or group achieve the success they desire, all while laughing along the way.

Book Honorée as your Keynote Speaker and you're guaranteed to make your event highly energizing and valuable!

For more information visit www.HonoreeCorder.com/speaking

Made in the USA
Las Vegas, NV
23 August 2021